ACCOUNTING FOR THE NUMBERPHOBIC

Accounting for the Numberphobic

A Survival Guide for Small Business Owners

DAWN FOTOPULOS

AMACOM
American Management Association
New York • Atlanta • Brussels • Chicago • Mexico City • San Francisco
Shanghai • Tokyo • Toronto • Washington, D. C.

Bulk discounts available. For details visit:
www.amacombooks.org/go/specialsales
Or contact special sales:
Phone: 800-250-5308
Email: specialsls@amanet.org
View all the AMACOM titles at: www.amacombooks.org
American Management Association: www.amanet.org

This publication is designed to provide accurate and authoritative information in regard to the subject matter covered. It is sold with the understanding that the publisher is not engaged in rendering legal, accounting, or other professional service. If legal advice or other expert assistance is required, the services of a competent professional person should be sought.

Library of Congress Cataloging-in-Publication Data
Fotopulos, Dawn.
    Accounting for the numberphobic : a survival guide for small business owners / Dawn Fotopulos.
        pages cm
    Includes bibliographical references and index.
    ISBN-13: 978-0-8144-3432-1
    ISBN-10: 0-8144-3432-0
    1. Small business—Management.   2. Small business—Accounting.   3. Managerial accounting.   I. Title.
    HD62.7.F67 2014
    657'.9042—dc23   2014003376

About AMA
American Management Association (www.amanet.org) is a world leader in talent development, advancing the skills of individuals to drive business success. Our mission is to support the goals of individuals and organizations through a complete range of products and services, including classroom and virtual seminars, webcasts, webinars, podcasts, conferences, corporate and government solutions, business books and research. AMA's approach to improving performance combines experiential learning—learning through doing—with opportunities for ongoing professional growth at every step of one's career journey.

Printing number
10 9 8 7 6 5 4 3 2 1

To **Katherine**, who always found an encouraging word for the struggling

CONTENTS

ACKNOWLEDGMENTS

Now I know for every book that is published, there is a silent army who helped give it life.

Frances Pelzman Liscio, you are the quintessential Renaissance woman and without you, this book would never have seen the light of day. You were the catalyst who set this book in motion. To a network of wonderful women I was lucky enough to be introduced to—Liza Dawson, Debbie Englander, Christina Parisi: thank you for helping me find my way to AMACOM.

To Senior Acquisitions Editor Bob Nirkind: Bob, thank you for believing in this project and for being so faithful to its completion. You wrestled mightily with each chapter and improved the book no end. Your patience and insights were a once-in-a-lifetime gift to a new author.

Dear Debbie Posner, my copyeditor, thank you for holding me to the highest standard. Knowing you has made me a better thinker, writer, and teacher. Your meticulous attention to detail and appetite for just a little mischief made a good book sing. You also made a grueling process a pleasure.

Mike Sivilli and the entire production team, thank you for your commitment and creativity in transforming this manuscript into a book that's ready for prime time.

Ron Bucalo, your illustrations are pure genius. They gave a dry topic a personality that invites the reader to understand so much more. No one can remain phobic while they're laughing. It is a joy working with a pro.

Dr. Lynne Rosansky, thank you for confirming that my mission is to teach financial literacy to the small business community and to Carole Hyatt for introducing us. My thanks to Susan RoAne, my book doula, and to Allison Armerding, who helped craft the proposal that was accepted against all odds.

To my Assistant Provost, Ina Kumi, thank you for the encouragement to keep plowing the land when the rocks were heavy and my arms were weak. To Dr. Anthony Bradley, thank you for poking me in the ribs for five years to get off the mark. Jacqueline Grey, thank you for keeping me vertical through one of the toughest 15-week slogs of my professional life. Valerie Coleman Morris, thank you for always reminding me to "just breathe" and for your unwavering faith I had something important to offer the world.

Jody Wood, your support during the early days of seminars on Accounting for the Numberphobic was a treasure. You told me to pay attention and I have. To Victoria Aviles, Gerta Hagen, Enid Karpeh, Nina Kaufman, Alexandra Preate, Laura Reddy, and Mike Zumchak, you've been true believers from the beginning and rabid fans. It's mutual.

To my cheering squad Lourine Clark, Philip Clements, Lucy De-Vismes, Marsha Heisler, Joanne Highly, Marleny Hucks, Roz Kroney, Monika Muller, Carla Rood, Anna Roundtree, and Michelle Turner. Your prayers sustained me on this unchartered journey.
Thank you Jane Applegate, CEO of the Applegate Group; Larry Janesky, CEO of Basement Systems; and April Vergara, SVP of HSBC

Bank. You are proof integrity and perseverance wins in a competitive world.

A special thanks to you, Norm Brodsky, for investing so much time to provide your searing insights. This book is much richer because of them.

Lee and Allie Hanley, your generosity of spirit is world-class. It's an honor to know you and to co-labor with you. You will always have my heartfelt gratitude.

To my beloved students of The King's College and the hundreds of participants I've had the privilege to coach through the Kauffman FastTrac Program at the Levin Institute in New York City, you are the inspiration hidden in these pages.

To God, who used the trial of a broken ankle to keep me focused on completing this manuscript in record time, thank you.

Thank you to my parents, Bill and Christine, who lived the mountaintop and valley experiences of Bedazzled so many years ago before I understood all this. I would have failed without you.

Most of all, thank you, dear reader, for picking up this book. May you finally grasp the success you've always known was waiting for you.

Why You Need This Book

When I say the words "financial statements," what goes through your mind? C'mon, be honest. Take a minute and write down your unscreened thoughts. It is okay if four-letter epithets come to mind. No one will see this but you.

Here are some comments written over the years by attendees of my workshop "I Hate Numbers: Accounting for the Numberphobic":

"Makes me want to get in the fetal position and cry."

"I'd rather spend a weekend listening to my mother-in-law."

"I hate numbers and they hate me. It's mutual."

"That's my accountant's problem."

"I'm a designer. I can't be bothered."

"If I work hard enough, the numbers will take care of themselves."

"The great black hole."

"Keeps me up at night."

"Someone shoot me, please!"

"I love reading my financial statements. I also love getting a flat tire on the highway in the pouring rain at 2 A.M. and getting my wisdom teeth extracted."

The people who made these comments are very smart, well educated, and talented—just like you. They are designers, IT consultants, photographers, dentists, lawyers, and even pole dancers for fitness. If you're intimidated by the numbers, you're in good company. Unfortunately, it happens to be the company of small businesspeople, many of whom are setting their businesses up to struggle and even fail.

Who will benefit from this book? People who run small businesses that sell products or services, accountants who have small business clients, salespeople, marketing people, subcontractors, next-generation small business managers, and entrepreneurs just starting out. Anyone who is thinking of striking out on his or her own, and wants to do it right, and anyone who has already taken the plunge and is struggling to pay the bills. Even the number-savvy—accountants, bookkeepers, receivables and payables clerks—will benefit. Their jobs will become much easier as their clients and customers learn the basics of small business survival.

SMALL BUSINESSES FAIL BECAUSE THEY ARE NOT ADEQUATELY FINANCED? NOT TRUE!

You've probably heard the Small Business Administration statistic that roughly half of small businesses launched in the United States never see their fourth year of operation. If you ask the experts in

Gucci loafers specializing in the painfully obvious, most tell you these businesses fail because they are not adequately capitalized. They cry, "These businesses need credit lines, loans, venture capital, angel investors, and government subsidies!" I beg to differ. There's plenty of the green stuff to go around. Just imagine how much in second-home mortgage money gets torched on ill-conceived businesses, useless online products, and just plain old clueless management. Billions of dollars have been thrown down the tubes in the last 20 years.

Every banker, consultant, and accountant I've spoken with agrees that most small businesses fail due to *management ignorance*, not undercapitalization. Start-up funds for most small businesses are not used to purchase equipment and build websites. They are used to pay for the management's learning curve—if the money doesn't run out before they break even.

So what exactly are small businesspeople ignorant about? It's not their product or service. Most people start or run a small business because they have great products and services and are world-class at what they do. But these qualities are not enough to build and manage a profitable enterprise. Without a well-maintained engine to deliver products and services, and without the management skills to maneuver and navigate that vehicle, any business will quickly stall out. This is where the numbers come in.

Many small businesspeople assume that numbers are the province of number experts—accountants. They don't realize that an accountant's role is similar to your car mechanic's. CPAs know all about the metrics and gauges that measure business operations and health. They can provide plenty of helpful information for performing "routine maintenance" on your business and helping you avoid the crosshairs of the IRS. But at the end of the day, your CPA is not going to manage your business any more than your mechanic is going to drive your car. You are the one who needs to know how to read your "financial dashboard" so you can get where you want to go.

Yes, learning to drive is daunting at first. But gas gauges, speedometers, engine lights, maps, and steering wheels are not rocket science—and neither are your financial statements. Learning to read them and use the information they provide to steer your business toward profitability is absolutely within your capabilities. Not only that, but you can master these skills much more quickly and easily than you imagine—as I will prove to you in this book.

No, you probably won't hear this from your CPA. He or she is happy to keep charging you $250 an hour to handle the "complicated stuff" that terrifies you. You're only going to hear it from someone like me—someone who learned how important it is to tackle the numbers, and ultimately, how feasible it really is.

I happen to be one of those (formerly) numberphobic small businesspeople who paid dearly for my own learning curve. I started a business at age 23 and almost went bankrupt several times. That is a 10-antacids-a-day-for-10-years way to learn about controlling things like the cost of goods—years of pain I wouldn't wish on anyone. Preventing that experience is my mission with this book. I'm confident that I can teach you in weeks what took me long, hard years to understand, just as I have taught hundreds of small businesspeople in my courses and seminars. My students constantly tell me, "You reached me!" "Now I know exactly what I need to do." "I've heard dozens of people talk about this stuff. I've never understood it until now." Many have come to me with tears in their eyes because, armed with the knowledge I share in this book, they knew their days of hopeless struggle were behind them. Hundreds of businesses that were ready to close their doors are now profitable and growing as a result of what's captured between these few pages.

HOW TO THINK ABOUT THIS BOOK

Have you ever watched the classic movie *The Wizard of Oz*? Do you remember the scene when Dorothy, the Scarecrow, the Lion, and the Tin Man were shivering in their shoes in front of the Great and Powerful Wizard? Flames were rising, his voice was booming, and the great hall rang out with his fierce and foreboding presence. Then, to Dorothy's horror, her little dog Toto ran over to the curtain behind the Wizard, grabbed a corner, and pulled it aside to reveal a powerless little man with a white beard from Kansas. The Great and Powerful Oz was cut down to size in an instant.

In the same way, *Accounting for the Numberphobic* is going to rip away all the smoke and bluster and show what's really behind the screen when it comes to using your financial statements to make great management decisions. It's going to nuke your numberphobia for good and leave you talking about business accounting as something "fun" and "easy." I know it sounds too good to be true. But after you read this book and review the "Key Takeaways" at the end of each chapter, which offer you the opportunity to apply concepts immediately and effectively, you'll see that managing a small business can be as easy as playing a video game—because you finally know how to keep score. This book efficiently lays out a tried-and-true roadmap for building a profitable business. This is my goal; I want to show you the simplest way to get there with a book that is comprehensive without being textbook-long or textbook-boring.

You may have taken accounting courses but this is not like any accounting book you've ever read. There's not one syllable with "debit," "credit," or GAAP lingo camouflaged on these pages. There are plenty of CPAs out there who have written the equivalent of nontoxic sleeping aids, so this book is easy to follow and fun to read.

Step by step, story by story, I make the hard things easy to understand and to implement. All roads are far easier to travel if they've already been paved.

Accounting for the Numberphobic begins by unpacking your three most important navigational tools line by line: the Net Income Statement (or Profit and Loss Statement), the Cash Flow Statement, and the Balance Sheet. Crucial to the very survival of your small business is understanding what these financial statements are telling you about the state of your business. Chapters 1 through 3 review the Net Income Statement, what it measures, how it works, and how you can improve profitability by making small changes. Chapter 4 takes you through a breakeven analysis, which is important to know if you're building a viable business. Chapters 5 and 6 contain in-the-trenches advice about reading your Cash Flow Statement and managing the collections process to avoid bankruptcy, something many business managers learn after it's too late.

Chapters 7 and 8 then focus on the Balance Sheet, how it works, and its importance in measuring the health of any small business. They'll make you an insider by showing you how bankers scrutinize the information on this statement and how you can use this insight to your advantage. Chapter 9 reveals how the Net Income Statement, Cash Flow Statement, and Balance Sheet interrelate as the business conducts day-to-day transactions. Eventually, these statements will become so second-nature to you that you'll be able to anticipate improvements or see risks before they happen. Chapter 10 reviews the key takeaways from the entire book through a once-in-a-lifetime interview with successful serial entrepreneur Norman Brodsky.

I want you to gain knowledge and wisdom. Knowledge is being able to look at a thermometer, for example, and see that it's 95 degrees outside. However, knowledge only benefits you when combined with wisdom. Wisdom tells you to wear shorts and flip-flops when you go out in 95-degree weather, instead of your snowsuit. Unfortunately, most training in business accounting focuses on knowledge rather than wisdom. I've met business owners who received an A in their undergraduate accounting courses and could define every last item on their financials, yet had no idea that if their gross margin fell below 30 percent, their business would be on the fast track to bankruptcy.

Financial statements measure events that have already happened and establish where you are right now. The great challenge as a small business manager is to gain the wisdom to use these data to identify opportunities, manage risks as they happen, and predict what will happen to the business in the future if you make certain decisions today.

WHY SHOULD YOU LISTEN TO DAWN FOTOPULOS?

I have spent over 20 years in business as a Wall Street trader; I worked as a Vice President in the Consumer Bank at Citigroup, where I ran the Marketing Group for Corporate Card Products, the fastest growing and most profitable product line in the institution at that time; and I was a serial entrepreneur for many, many years. I have also successfully launched more than 80 businesses and product lines across a spectrum of industries including financial services, consumer products, real-estate development, high technology, and nonprofits.

I'm currently an Associate Professor of Business at The King's College in Manhattan, where I teach principles of management, business strategy, and introduction to marketing, and have been a visiting speaker at Columbia Business School, an adjunct professor at the Stern School of Business at New York University, and a certified facilitator for the Kauffman FastTrac® programs for entrepreneurs.

In addition, I'm a CEO Leader of the national organization Job Creator's Alliance, started by Home Depot founder Bernie Marcus. My role is to conduct monthly media appearances to advocate for policies that support new business formation and job creation.

I am the founder of Best Small Biz Help.com, my award-winning blog and resource site, whose mission is to ensure that small businesspeople increase profits with limited resources in any economy. The "Panic Button" helpdesk on the site provides live research on what the pressures are that face our target audience: small businesspeople.

My extensive experience diagnosing sick companies across every major industry in the market has been invaluable to both students and small businesses. There's no faking a deep understanding of how complex and challenging it is to run a successful small business.

* * *

Don't be misled by the title of this book: *Accounting for the Numberphobic* is not just about the numbers, accounting, or financial statements. It's about the future of your business. It's about equipping you to get adequately compensated for your talent so you can support your family and household. It's about leveraging your skills, gifts, and experience to have something tangible to show for all your hard work and sleepless nights. It's about giving you a roadmap so your small business does not become a statistic like 50 percent of your peers. It's about giving people who run small businesses—whether from an office or a storefront, from the basement, garage, or dining room table—the freedom to dream again and for that dream to become a reality no matter what the roller-coaster economy is doing.

This book is on a mission: to teach you how to keep score by reading your basic financials and understanding what they are telling you to do. Then running a small business can actually become fun and not terrifying. You will be able to anticipate the future instead of becoming a victim of it. When the bills come in, you'll have the cash to pay them. Most important, you'll have a business strategy for achieving business success.

WHAT YOU'LL LEARN

- Your financial dashboard is the key to keeping track; it is key to measuring your progress. Learn how to use it to make wise decisions.

- You run the business on gross margin, not on revenues. Work half as hard and increase profits.

- A small business can show a profit and still be going bankrupt. We'll show you how to avoid this.

- You must collect on outstanding invoices. This book makes it painless.

- Experts who have weathered the storm of small business management give you priceless advice that will set you on the path to profit in any economy.

Whether you are currently in the trenches or have just the barest glimmer of an idea, you will gain immeasurably from these pages.

So you have two choices. You can let the numbers continue to intimidate you, leaving you forever enslaved to expensive advisors, or you can read this book, conquer your fears, and learn how to drive a business down the exhilarating and rewarding road to profitability and positive, predictable cash flow. Whether you're a small business dreamer, owner, manager, or supplier, you need to know what's between these pages. While other companies struggle, yours can rise above the fray and flourish. That's my prayer for you. So let's get started by learning how to track profits through the Net Income Statement.

ACCOUNTING FOR THE NUMBERPHOBIC

CHAPTER **1**

Your Financial Dashboard

The Net Income Statement, Cash Flow
Statement, and Balance Sheet

Accounting is a *really* big, complicated subject. It's no surprise that many small business managers want to hand anything to do with numbers off to the "number people"—CPAs, bookkeepers, bankers, and tax lawyers. Perhaps you can relate. If terms like GAAP accounting principles, tax legislation, debits and credits, and tax forms stress you out, don't worry. First, you're not alone. Second, this book is not going to cover these topics. It is, however, going to confront you with a truth you cannot afford to deny: *If you want to be successful at managing a business, you need to become proficient at handling certain numbers. Put simply, you need to be able to read and understand your financial dashboard.*

Think about the dashboard in your car. You have a speedometer, a gas gauge, and an oil pressure gauge. These instruments measure the vital signs of your car's operation.

They give you critical information about how fast you're moving, how much fuel you have in your tank, and the state of your engine. If any one of these instruments isn't functioning or you don't know how to read it, then pretty soon you're going to be getting a ticket, stalling out, or blowing a gasket.

Similarly, your **financial dashboard** has three gauges you need to be able to read to manage a business—your Net Income Statement, your Cash Flow Statement, and your Balance Sheet. These statements measure the vital signs of your business operations. They provide you with critical information about how much profit the business is generating, how much cash you have in the bank to run the business, and the overall health of the business at a point in time—information that allows you to make wise and timely decisions that will keep the business humming like a tuned-up car. And guess what? Your bookkeeper isn't going to make those decisions for you. He's there to make sure you have accurate and timely records of business transactions to send to your CPA. Your CPA is not going to make those decisions either. She is there to prepare your taxes and make sure you don't get audited.

It's entirely possible for your "number people" to be doing their jobs superbly while you are steering your business into a financial danger zone. You could be spending money on the wrong things. As a business manager, you might be taking out crazy amounts of debt without understanding how fast that can sink the business. *You are the one in the driver's seat.* And if you can't read your financial dashboard, you're driving with your eyes blindfolded.

Unfortunately, this is exactly what over 85 percent of small business managers are doing, according to the U.S. Small Business Administration. It's no wonder that 40 percent of these businesses fail to survive even four years. If you've heard this statistic, you've probably also heard the reasoning that it must be due to lack of start-up cash or unviable products and services. It's not. There is plenty of cash available and broad enough markets for the business you manage to find new and loyal customers. Small businesses largely fail due to *mismanagement*. If you want to keep the business out of bankruptcy and reach the most important destination—sustainable profits and free cash flow—then you need to take the basic driving lessons necessary to maneuver a profit-making vehicle for the products or services you manage. You need to become fluent in reading what the financial dashboard reveals about your business.

The great news is that you're entirely capable of becoming an expert at this. How do I know? Because I've taught hundreds of small business managers—including the most extreme of number phobics—what I'm about to teach you. I've seen them grasp the concepts easily and, with many wonderful "aha!" moments, immediately begin to see exactly where the risks and opportunities are because they can finally understand how to respond to the numbers on their Net Income Statement, Cash Flow Statement, and Balance Sheet.

My objective in this chapter is to expand your financial vocabulary beyond "bankruptcy" and "billionaire." If you are like most small business managers, you may be familiar with some, if not most, of the financial terms in this book, but be at a total loss when it comes to grasping their meaning and real-world implications. This is like driving down the highway without being able to read the road signs. When you see a sign with the number "65" on it, there are several levels of knowledge you must have in order to read it. You need to know that it's a speed limit, and that you're expected to make sure the needle on your speedometer stays on or under a corresponding "65" mark. You also need to know what this sign implies: If you exceed this speed limit, you risk getting a speeding ticket. You may even lose your license if you test the limits too frequently.

The numbers on your financial documents are like that speed limit sign. The sign doesn't need to communicate everything— you've been taught what it means, and if you've been driving for a while, and especially if you've ever gotten a speeding ticket, then you know its implications. The sign is small, but the meaning is significant. The same is true of those little numbers on your financial dashboard. There are some nuances and calibrations to learn that are essential to you as you make day-to-day business decisions.

So let's start learning the lingo. I'm going to start by giving you a basic overview of these three financial documents and what they measure, along with a brief introduction to some of the implications these measurements have for managing your business. Let's start with your speedometer—the Net Income Statement.

THE NET INCOME STATEMENT

The **Net Income Statement**, also known as the "Income State-ment," "Profit and Loss Statement," and "P&L," reveals whether a business is generating a profit, breaking even, or showing a loss. If you didn't know that, don't worry. Many small business managers don't know it either. One small business manager who ran a series of salons for children attended one of my seminars. When I told her that all these terms mean exactly the same thing, she jumped up and said, "Are you kidding me? Is *that* what my accountant's been talking about all these years?"

Accountants might refer to the Net Income Statement as the "Income Statement," typically dropping the qualifier "Net" because it's implied and they assume you know that. And now you actually do. Similarly, the terms "net revenue" and "revenue" are used interchangeably. And sometimes you may see either "revenue" or "revenues" used as the plural form to describe the total amount of net sales. None of these terms should leave you in the cold.

By the way, whenever you see the qualifier "**gross**"—such as gross profits, gross receipts, or gross revenue—it means you're looking at those numbers *before* expenses or discounts are deducted. Anytime you see the qualifier "**net**"—as in net revenue, net expenses, or net income—it means you're looking at the numbers *after* certain expenses have been accounted for. Armed with this simple knowledge, you're already way ahead of the pack.

Here are the key questions the Net Income Statement answers for you as a small business manager:

- Is our business making any money?

- Are our products and services the right ones?

- Are we pricing our products and services so that we're not cheating ourselves out of a reasonable return while still remaining an attractive alternative to the competition?

- Is our gross margin robust enough to run the business?

- Do we know what our true direct costs are?

- How do we know our marketing efforts are paying off?

- Do we have the right mix of clients?

- How can we work half as hard and make twice the money?

The Net Income Statement will reveal whether your business is generating a profit, breaking even, or losing money. If the number on the bottom line is positive, you're making money. If it's zero, you're breaking even. If it's negative, you're losing money. The bottom line is what's left after every direct and indirect expense is paid from net revenue. That number is why you're in business. It's net profit.

Why should you care whether your business is making a profit or not? Because when you run a small business, you're taking on a lot of risk. You're making enormous sacrifices in time and effort. I don't know about you, but if I'm working 12-hour days to keep the place running and my Net Income Statement isn't showing a profit, it puts me in a really bad mood. Some small business managers camp out in no-profit territory for months—others somehow hang on for stress-filled decades. Frankly, it's no mystery that over 40 percent of small businesses don't see their fourth year of operation. It's miraculous 60 percent do. Without sustained and growing profits, your small business may be spinning its wheels (at least at the moment), but it won't be *getting anywhere.*

In the next chapter, we'll be going over your Net Income Statement line by line so you can understand each of the factors influencing that number on the bottom line. You'll learn exactly where to start tinkering and adjusting when you see profits erode. Some of the primary areas we'll examine include the following (Don't worry—all of these and more will be discussed in further detail!):

- *Your pricing strategy.* Your prices have a direct effect on your bottom line—not only now, but in the future. How your business prices its talents, products, or services influences how many customers will buy. I'll teach you how to set your business' prices and how to recognize when it's time to change them.

- *Diversifying the client base.* Every client you sell to provides cash streams to the business, like a company in an investment portfolio. And just like a healthy investment portfolio, a healthy small business portfolio contains many clients, none of which represents more than 15 percent of the business's net revenue. This diversity mitigates risk by preventing any one client from jeopardizing the health of the business. Small business managers

must learn to target potential clients and manage existing clients so no one client can put a large portion of the
company's revenue at risk.

- *Gross margin (by product and by customer).* Most small
  business managers don't know that you don't run your
  business on revenue—you run it on **gross margin**,
  which is the gross profit available to pay all your operating expenses. Understanding gross margin is critical
  to the role you play in a small business. If you don't understand it, you may keep products or services that, in
  fact, should be dropped because they're losing money.
  You may keep clients that buy only the lowest margined
  products or services because you have no idea that
  every time they buy, *they cost the business money.* You
  may even have a problem paying the bills and you won't
  know why. Most small business managers try to solve
  this problem by selling more, but only end up digging
  the business into a deeper financial hole. You'll learn
  how to make strategic adjustments to products and
  clients so you can avoid this trap.

- *Fixed and variable expenses.* Like revenue, not all expenses are created equal. Not only will you understand
  the difference, but you'll learn simple strategies that will
  help you manage expenses effectively as your business
  grows.

- *Marketing costs and return on investment.* Small business managers are wasting millions of dollars on ill-
  conceived marketing programs, praying something will
  stick. The "spray and pray" strategy never works. At a
  small business conference, an advertiser asked me what
  my marketing budget was in an attempt to sell me a

very pricey marketing program. I responded that this was an irrelevant question and suggested he ask me instead how many customers I needed, of what type, within what time frame, and what it would take to reach them. Only then could we have an intelligent conversation about how to strategically build a marketing program and how to get and measure a return on my investment. In the chapters ahead, you'll learn to see how your business's marketing is really affecting its bottom line so you can protect and grow its profits.

As you'll discover, there are many ways to increase a business's profits, and some of them can be implemented more quickly and easily than you can imagine. These approaches have turned around hundreds of failing businesses. As you utilize the strategies in this book, you'll not only boost your profitability in the short term, you'll begin to predict what will happen to profits in the long term thanks to the actions you're taking today. You'll make better business decisions. You'll make faster course corrections before a crisis hits. You'll be more resilient than the competition when the market around you is roiling. This is the biggest key to long-term small business success.

As I said, your Net Income Statement is like the speedometer in your car. It's the gauge you're going to want to check frequently—

at least every 30 days—to make sure you're maintaining healthy momentum. It lets you know if profits are increasing or decreasing. Keep in mind profits will fluctuate monthly because there is a seasonality to sales and that's to be expected. The real challenge is to anticipate those high- and low-profit months so the business can always pay its expenses and stay viable.

However, your Net Income Statement—your speedometer—is not going to tell you how much further you'll be able to go before you need to put gas in your tank. So now let's talk about your gas gauge: the Cash Flow Statement.

THE CASH FLOW STATEMENT

Unless you want to be left on the side of the road, you know it's a pretty good idea to keep your eye on the needle of your gas gauge. That needle ranges between two points—"F" for "Full" and "E" for "Empty." Think about it. The gas gauge does *not* tell you that you need to buy more gas if the needle is closer to "E." It's up to *you* to figure that out, or suffer the consequences. It's also up to you to know that your particular automobile can go a certain distance on a tank of gas. If you own an eight-cylinder, 400-horsepower SUV, for example, then you know your car drinks gas like college freshmen guzzle beer.

Cash is to your business as gasoline is to your car. Every business, like every car, will burn cash at different rates.

But you need to *measure it* and not guess. Guessing is the HOV lane to bankruptcy. When you run out of cash, it's game over.

Your **Cash Flow Statement**, as the name indicates, measures the flow of cash in and out of your business. This gauge works like your personal checkbook. You start (one can only hope) with a positive cash balance at the beginning of the month. Cash comes in from customer payments, investments, or loans. Cash goes out to pay bills and salaries. Your ending cash is brought forward to begin the cycle again in the following month.

There are three primary sources of cash for small businesses, and they are not all created equal. You can get cash from operations, from bank loans (which must be paid back), or from investors (who take a pound of flesh in equity for it). Cash from operations is your premium fuel. That's cash generated directly from selling products or services to customers at a profit and getting paid for them. It has no interest cost attached to it. You don't have to pay it back. You don't have to use it to feed hungry investors. You earned it. This cash belongs to the business for the owners and managers to allocate as they see fit. The business should get compensated for all the risks involved in offering products and services throughout both strong and soft economic environments.

That said, there are several factors influencing whether that wonderful premium fuel will make it into your business's gas tank *in time* to keep it from hitting "E." Here are some aspects of your business that you need to learn to fine-tune if you want to build and sustain healthy cash flow from operations:

- *Your invoicing policy.* Most small business managers take this for granted, but invoicing can be a client-relationship builder or destroyer. It is also mission critical for maximizing cash flow. If you've perfected your pricing and are showing great sales but aren't getting your customers to pay you quickly enough, you're going to be in trouble. In a slow market, getting paid takes longer, particularly when you're doing business with companies that buy volume up front and pay later. In Chapter 5, I'll show you simple and creative ways to collect against your invoices and build strong, lasting customer relationships. This will make a tremendous difference on how much cash you have to invest in your business at the end and beginning of every month. It will strengthen your ability to pay your bills even when revenue is weak, and make you less vulnerable to providers of outside sources of cash that rarely offer terms in your favor.

- *Collections policies.* When you manage a business, you're a collections agent, whether you like it or not. Collecting money from deadbeat clients is often as pleasant as having a root canal. Collections policies should not be afterthoughts. They should be communicated up front and in ways that strengthen long-term customer relationships. Most small business managers have no concept of how to do this productively and what the consequences are if they don't. In Chapters 5, 6, and 10 you'll learn several ways to improve your policies and your cash flow dramatically with minimal scarring.

- *Credit extensions.* How trusting many small business managers are! Once they get the purchase order signed, they're so excited that they don't realize that what they've just done is hand the keys to the kingdom over to the client. Chapter 6 will help you become very savvy about extending credit and managing the downside risk—and there *is* a downside risk, trust me.

- *Dealing with suppliers.* Suppliers are a key part of the value chain for any small business, especially if the products or services they provide are mission critical. But if your small business doesn't represent a large portion of a supplier's revenue, you run the risk of being treated like a toxic fungus. (I exaggerate, but you may well find yourself relegated to the back of the line, with nuisance status.) In Chapter 6, you'll learn how to manage payment expectations with clients and to negotiate favorable payment terms with suppliers.

- *Dealing with the bank.* You may not know this, but the bank is not your friend. Prime-time commercials say otherwise, but the truth comes out when you submit an application for a loan. Suddenly, you find you've fallen down the rabbit hole in a Lewis Carroll fantasy. As a former banker, I will show you the world from the bank's perspective and coach you on how to keep a tight rein on the borrowed streams of cash in your cash flow. Chapter 8 takes you through a simple analysis that could transform the banking relationship for any small business.

In coming chapters, you'll see Cash Flow Statements from businesses just like the one you're running—whether a product business or a service business—and see how they can improve. It won't take long for you to become an astute diagnostician when looking at this cash gauge on your dashboard. You'll soon be making easy, strategic maneuvers that can improve your cash flow from operations almost overnight.

Here are some basic questions your Cash Flow Statement will answer:

- Does my business have enough cash to pay its bills for the next three months?

- What expenses can I reduce dramatically and which ones are mission critical to the business?

- How do I plan for cash needs during the lean months of the year?

- When is the best time to apply for a credit line and how do I manage it?

THE BALANCE SHEET

Last but not least, let's turn to the oil pressure gauge on our financial dashboard, the Balance Sheet. This statement might not seem too interesting at first, but to your banker or a lender, this statement is sexier than a string bikini. If you want to know the overall health and financial strength of any business, the Balance Sheet will reveal it easily, if you know how to read it. Your **Balance Sheet** captures all the outstanding loans and debt or liabilities incurred by the business since its inception, the value of all your business's assets, and its net worth. Some assets are liquid (cash) and some are illiquid, or not easily converted into cash (buildings). Some assets are tangible property (product, equipment, etc.) and some are intangible (brand equity, good will).

You need to understand each of these assets and liabilities and how they influence the **net worth** of your business. Your net worth, shown on your Balance Sheet, is simply the difference between what your business owns and what it owes. (Net worth is sometimes referred to as "**owner's equity**," whether there is one owner or several.) That number can be positive or negative. As you've probably already guessed, a negative net worth means you owe more than you own.

A positive net worth is what you're after, for a couple of reasons. First, it makes you more attractive to banks if you do want and need to borrow cash. In Chapter 8, I'll give you an insider's view on how a banker will look at your Balance Sheet. I'll show you how the numbers should influence your decisions on when to get a loan and the kinds of loans you need to avoid if you don't want to fry your engine.

Second, a positive net worth positions a business to be sold if necessary or desired. Don't worry—
I won't bore you with the partic-
ulars of selling a business in
this book. But you do need to
prepare for this possibility, and
this means keeping track of
how much the business is
worth and which of its assets
are transferable. Much of this
information shows up on your
Balance Sheet.

You move toward positive
net worth in two basic ways—
driving asset values up and
driving liabilities down. Sometimes the economy is a big help here.
If you bought a home in 1990 and held onto it, that home, an asset,
improved in value just because demand was so strong. The asset
value increased, which increased your net worth without you having to do anything but maintain the structure. Driving liabilities
down is about making sure the business doesn't borrow more
money than it needs to as it grows. The same way a household can
take on some debt and still thrive, a business can do the same
thing. It's possible to reach the point of no return—when debt has
become so large that it becomes impossible to pay it back. Once
again, it's game over.

Sadly, a lot of small business managers are driving their asset
values down and their liabilities up and they don't even realize it.
In Chapter 7, you'll read numerous examples of how smart, well-
meaning managers have found very creative ways to diminish their
asset values, take on crippling debt, and ultimately destroy every-

thing they've worked for all their lives. I'll show you exactly how to avoid their fate.

Here are some of the questions you want to be asking as you read your Balance Sheet:

- Does the business have too much debt?

- Is it getting a good return on the debt it is carrying?

- Does the business have the right kind of debt?

- Are asset values growing or shrinking relative to liabilities?

- How much working capital does the business have?

- Does the business have too much or too little inventory?

* * *

Hopefully this introduction to your financial dashboard has given you an inkling that it might be worth your time to get fluent in the language of the Net Income Statement, the Cash Flow Statement, and the Balance Sheet. In Chapter 9, I'll bring it all together and explain how each of these statements relates to one another. You'll also see how, after reviewing all three, every business manager has the potential to make better decisions to drive stronger profits, a more adequate cash flow, and increased net worth for a business. Chapter 10 is an interview with famed entrepreneur Norman Brodsky who shares a lifetime's worth of advice on how to run a more successful small business.

I know very well that, like any small business manager, you're strapped for time. But I also know that reading this book is one of the best time investments you'll ever make in learning to manage a small business. Do yourself and the world a favor by refusing to join the thousands of other incredibly talented and innovative people with excellent ideas, services, and products who have ended up

crashed or stalled out in the ditches of commerce. This book will demystify basic principles you can apply today to improve profits, cash flow, and net worth.

KEY TAKEAWAYS

▶ Three key statements that make up your financial dashboard to help keep track of the health of the business: the Net Income Statement, the Cash Flow Statement, and the Balance Sheet.

▶ The Net Income Statement reveals whether a business is generating a profit, breaking even, or showing a loss. It should be reviewed by the manager every month after the monthly books are reconciled by the bookkeeper or accountant. It will show how the business has performed that month.

▶ Profits will fluctuate month to month due to seasonal changes in demand for various products and services. Try to maintain positive profits by the end of each quarter.

▶ The Cash Flow Statement measures the inflows and outflows of cash from operations. From this statement, you'll know whether the business can pay its expenses next month or next quarter. This statement will also reveal how long the business can be sustained without additional sources of cash. The most successful small business managers I've met look at their Cash Flow Statements weekly. Cash levels are key.

▶ The Balance Sheet captures the full results of business operations since the beginning. It's a snapshot of the health of the business at a moment in time. Assets (what is owned by the business) minus liabilities (what is owed by the business) reveals owner's equity—the net worth—of the company.

▶ An increase in asset values and a decrease in liabilities means net worth is improving. This should be one of your goals.

CHAPTER 2

The Net Income Statement

The Key to Growing Your Profits

As you saw in Chapter 1, the first question your financial dashboard answers is whether or not the business is making a profit. Your Net Income Statement reveals the answer to this burning question.

The bird's-eye view of the Net Income Statement breaks down as follows:

- **Net revenue** (This is sales less any discounts; it's the money coming into your company.)

- Less: **Cost of goods sold** (These are your direct product or service costs.)

- **Gross margin** (This is what's left before operating expenses.)

- Less: **Fixed expenses** (These are expenses like rent.)

- Less: **Variable expenses** (These are expenses like marketing.)

- **Earnings before taxes (EBT)**

- Less: **Taxes** (These are expenses you can't forget to pay!)

- **Net income** (This is what's left for the business—the bottom line. This number reveals if the business is profitable and how large that profit is.)

So, once again: Net revenue minus COGS equals gross margin. Gross margin minus expenses (fixed and variable) equals EBT. EBT minus taxes equals net income. This seems very straightforward, but then, I've been trained in the trenches. The important thing—the reason for this book—is that it must become straightforward to *you*.

LINE ITEMS ON YOUR NET INCOME STATEMENT

To help personalize the experience of reading a Net Income Statement, I'll put you in my business "simulator." Congratulations! You are now the manager of a very creative company called Bedazzled, Inc. This is the name of my first small business when I was young, foolish, and, like most small business owners, had no clue how to read a Net Income Statement! Stories from that experience—O Youth, whither wentest thou?—are sprinkled throughout this book. I'm hoping that my mistakes may illuminate your decision-making process.

So, what do you do as Bedazzled's spanking new manager? You screen-print marvelous beach cover-ups, which you sell by the thousands to some high-profile retailers and boutiques. Let's see how Bedazzled's net revenue is doing by looking at the individual line items on its Net Income Statement.

Net Revenue

You may have heard your CPA or some financial insider refer to your "top line." They're talking about that first line on your Net Income Statement. (Don't you love it when something makes sense?) Your top line is your **net revenue**. It's how much you've sold for that month, less any discounts you may have offered customers. For our purposes, this number is the same as net sales. Every time you ring the cash register or invoice a client, net revenue goes up. It's a beautiful thing when money comes into your business. (For the purists out there, I acknowledge there might be other sources of revenue for a business, like interest income, but we're keeping it simple and assuming net revenue and net sales are the same thing.)

Calculating net revenue for Bedazzled, Inc. is quite simple. Multiply how many T-shirts were sold by how much you charged for each one. Here it is in shorthand:

$$(\# \text{ T-shirts sold}) \times (\text{Unit Price}) = \text{Net Revenue}$$

So, if one T-shirt is sold for $10.00, then net revenue is $10.00. If 1,000 T-shirts are sold for $10.00 each, net revenue is $10,000. That's pretty straightforward. If 10 clients buy different quantities of T-shirts and the task is to determine total revenue, just add all the subtotals up from each sale, and you'll get total net revenue for the month. All desktop or cloud software solutions will do this for you automatically. Someone in the business, either the owner, the manager, or the bookkeeper, just needs to enter each sale and deduct any discounts.

What if you have a product line with different T-shirts at different prices? Say, for example, that you offer one T-shirt with a butterfly design for $12.00 and a T-shirt with a seashell design for $15.00. Let's compare two orders from two different customers:

- Customer A buys 20 T-shirts: 10 butterflies and 10 seashells. How much in total revenue did Customer A generate?

10 butterflies × $12.00 = $120

10 seashells × $15.00 = $150

Total Revenue from Customer A = $270

- Customer B buys 20 seashell T-shirts. How much in total revenue did Customer B generate?

20 seashells × $15.00 = $300

Total Revenue from Customer B = $300

Aha! Customer B bought the *very same number of T-shirts, yet generated more in revenue*—$30.00 more, to be exact. Why? Because each seashell T-shirt was a little more expensive than the butterfly T-shirt. Comparing the impact each customer has on your net revenue, it's clear that Customer B offers more to your top line than Customer A.

Don't be fooled, though. Even though Customer B paid more for your T-shirts, you still don't know if Customer B is more profitable than Customer A. We only have revenue or sales information. We haven't figured out how much each sale cost yet. This example illustrates a powerful truth: Just because one customer's purchases are *greater* than another's, it doesn't mean that this customer is *more profitable* for the business. (We'll be digging into the implications of this more.) A larger sales order doesn't necessarily mean greater profits because the T-shirts cost something to manufacture.

The direct cost to fabricate the shirts has to be deducted from the net revenue from each order to really know how profitable each sale is and each customer is. The next line on your Net Income

Statement—titled "Cost of Goods Sold"—will help identify which T-shirt design delivers the most gross margin (also known as "gross profit") for the business. Depending on which designs a customer buys, you'll be able to tell which customers are most profitable.

Cost of Goods Sold

Your **cost of goods sold (COGS)** is the total cost of the direct materials and direct labor used in the production of your products. In the case of the T-shirts, direct materials include things like fabric, yarn, and thread. Direct labor costs include screening the designs, cutting, and assembling the T-shirts. These are direct costs because they are the expenses required to build a finished product that is ready for sale. COGS is considered a *direct variable* cost because it varies with the number of units sold. These direct costs will look different for each product the business sells. For example, it just so happens that the seashell T-shirts require twice the amount of screen printing as the butterfly shirts, making them more expensive to manufacture. This means that the cost per unit for the seashell T-shirts is higher than the butterfly T-shirts.

It's absolutely essential to know the **unit cost** for every product the company sells. This is the direct cost of materials and labor required to create a saleable product whether that product has been sold or not. Unit cost is the same as COGS for product that has been sold and shipped out the door. Unit cost is also used to measure the value of **inventory**, which is product that's been made but not sold yet. A product's unit cost may fluctuate, due to external factors such as increases in the cost of raw materials or of labor. Once a product is sold, the sale will be captured as net revenue and unit cost will be reflected as COGS on the Net Income Statement. If product has been produced but not sold, it's considered inventory and the cost to produce it will be captured on the Balance Sheet, which we'll review in Chapter 7. If it's unclear what the unit cost is for each of your products, ask the accountant or bookkeeper to determine that number for you.

Knowing unit cost is essential because this is one of the key considerations when figuring out what should be charged for a product. (Other factors include your competition and operating expenses, but we'll cover all of that in Chapter 3.)

Your price must be *significantly* higher than your unit costs if a product is to be profitable. If, for example, your COGS for the seashell T-shirt was $15.00 and you set your price at $5.00, the business would be losing $10.00 on every T-shirt you sold. If those T-shirts really started to sell, the business would be draining savings faster than the federal government drains its annual budget! Selling more units doesn't lead to more profits if unit costs are too high or the selling price is too low—it actually leads to *losses*.

You may be asking, "Who in their right mind would sell something for less than it cost to make it?" I've exaggerated this example to make a point, but the truth is that far more businesspeople do this than you can imagine. Few small business managers know the true, fully loaded cost of goods of the products they are selling, so they're pricing the product based on false assumptions. Likewise, those who manage service businesses often fail to accurately calculate their costs, especially their time. Without knowing total direct costs, setting price becomes an expensive guess.

It's been my experience that the default is to set prices too low. Other business managers, in their desperation to find new customers, reduce the selling price below cost to entice anyone to buy. Just ask the people who use deep discounters, like Groupon, to find new customers. Almost all those businesses are losing big money on those promotions. And the customers they find are not loyal and rarely buy a second time at full price. The business loses money on the advertising expense and each product that's sold.

Now it's true that some businesses, at times, may need to price below cost. If a business sells perishable goods, out-of-season goods, or goods that quickly become technologically obsolete, it might make sense to sell inventory at a deep discount just to raise cash. Unless a business is selling rare diamonds or valuable antiques, most inventory decreases in value over time until it becomes worthless. It's better to get a few cents on the dollar than nothing at all. *But this should be the exception, not the rule.* The rule of thumb is to sell a product at COGS *plus* 45 percent, to make it worth the risk to offer that product. This will also help guarantee enough gross margin from each sale to pay for the operating expenses of the business. For example: If COGS is $5.00 per unit, our markup is 45 percent of $5.00, or $2.25, and we can easily solve for minimum selling price per unit.

$$(\$5.00 \text{ COGS per unit}) + (\$2.25)$$
$$= \text{Minimum Selling Price, or } \$7.25$$

The goal is to build a profitable business, not maintain an expensive hobby that will leave you in the poorhouse. Make sure the premium charged above costs is adequate to keep the business viable.

So what management decisions can be made if the price being charged for products does not adequately cover the cost to produce them? Here are three possibilities to restore profitability:

1. *Raise the unit price*, but only if customers are willing to pay for it.

2. *Lower the COGS* by re-engineering the product.

3. *Drop that product from the lineup* if it won't sell at a price high enough to cover the COGS plus a 45 percent premium.

If it's possible to raise unit price *and* lower COGS while maintaining sales, you've hit the jackpot! A solid, integrated marketing strategy might provide the way to do this. Just remember, if the business promotes products to increase sales when the unit price is too close to the product's cost, that business will sink into a deeper financial hole. Don't get caught in the trap of losing money on every sale and attempting to make it up in volume. That's never a viable option. Likewise, don't get caught hanging onto products that are not generating adequate gross margin.

Every product or service offered has to deliver *at least a 45 percent premium* above what it costs to make it or to deliver it. Forget about those products or services everyone wants but is unwilling to pay for, or the products *you* love but customers won't buy. They will kill the profit potential of the business.

Gross Margin

Okay, we've covered the first two lines on the Net Income Statement. You have a general idea of how net revenue is generated and calculated. You know what COGS is and how it should help determine unit prices. It's clear that prices charged must be at least 45 percent higher than the COGS if the goal is to deliver a positive bottom line, or net income, the sign the business is profitable. After we deduct COGS from net revenue we're left with gross margin, or gross profit, not net income. Why? Because gross margin hasn't accounted for all the expenses to run the business yet. "Gross margin" is also referred to as "contribution margin" or just "margin" for short. Just remember that "gross margin," "gross profit," "contribution margin," and "margin" all refer to the same thing—the premium that's left after COGS (unit cost) is deducted from net revenue. It's that 45 percent premium over unit costs discussed earlier. Although it may vary slightly from industry to industry, the hurdle rate for gross margin is that it be equal to or greater than 30 percent of the net revenue. If your gross margin is less than 30 percent of net revenue, the company may run into trouble.

The Net Income Statement is the only statement that measures gross margin, and it's critically important that you know this number. Why? *A business doesn't run on net revenue; it runs on gross margin.* The gross margin is what is used to pay all the operating or indirect expenses to keep the business humming. These expenses typically include (but are not limited to) rent, insurance, salaries (including your own!), other general and administrative expenses, professional fees (accountants and lawyers), and, last but not least, city, state, and federal taxes.

Say, for example, that each seashell T-shirt costs $5 to make. If each one is sold for $15, how much gross margin was made on each T-shirt?

$$\$15.00 \text{ (Unit Price)} - \$5.00 \text{ (Unit COGS)}$$
$$= \$10.00 \text{ Unit Gross Margin}$$

That means for every T-shirt sold, the business generates $10.00 to help pay all the operating expenses. If 1,000 T-shirts are sold with this same pricing and cost structure, the business will generate $10,000 in gross margin:

$$1,000 \text{ Units} \times \$10.00 \text{ Gross Margin per Unit}$$
$$= \$10,000 \text{ Gross Margin}$$

Now we've got some pocket change to run the company. Actually, more than just pocket change. I admit that these are wonderfully positive figures. (Bedazzled's T-shirts had copyrighted designs and were easily sold at a premium.) As it happens, having such a positive gross margin puts you miles ahead of some companies, including a few big ones.

Take, for example, the infamous Chevy Volt. When the Volt was first introduced, it cost General Motors $79,000 to make the car. That monstrous number did not include the engineering costs to design and develop the car, just the direct costs to manufacture it. Chevy set the retail price for the Volt at $49,000 to try to be competitive with other electric cars in its class. If you've been tracking, this means that the Volt generated a *negative* gross margin of $39,000 at launch.

GM did what you should avoid like the plague—selling a product at almost half the true cost to make it. At that rate, the government should have subsidized GM *not to make the car*. It might actually have been cheaper to keep the plants idle and pay employees full wages while saving the direct materials costs. Clearly, profitability was not the aim, but you get the idea.

Besides the massive negative gross margin, Chevy had another big problem. The Volt's retail price—$49,000—wasn't even in the same solar system as its competitor made by Toyota, which sold for $29,000. So not only did GM make a car it couldn't afford to sell, but customers would never buy the Volt because it had no hope of beating the competition. That's a product that fired on no cylinders. What does this story tell us? The unit price for a product must cover COGS plus a 45 percent premium—*and* that the retail price needs to be competitive with attractive options currently in the market.

Even the big companies can get it terribly wrong. Now you know what negative gross margin looks like in the automobile business.

Repeat after me: *Every product or service must have a gross margin of at least 30 percent of net revenue or 45 percent above cost of goods sold.*

You can get to gross margin two ways: by using net revenue per unit as the reference or by using COGS per unit as the reference. I prefer using the COGS method as a first line of approach, because you start with your true costs and add your premium. If you find this forces you to charge more than the market will bear, you will have a good handle on the process and can better figure out how to modify it (lower your costs) without sacrificing quality (and possibly hurting your brand) or of improving the value of the product or service so the higher retail price becomes worth it in the eyes of your prospective customers.

Using Net Revenue to Determine Maximum COGS and Minimum Gross Margin

Assume butterfly T-shirts sell for $12.00 each. That's $12.00 net revenue per shirt. The goal is for gross margin to be 30 percent of $12.00, or $3.60 per shirt. That means COGS can be no more than $8.40 per shirt.

Putting this another way, if 30 percent gross margin is the goal, COGS cannot be higher than 70 percent of selling price (net revenues).

Using COGS to Determine Selling Price and Minimum Gross Margin

The COGS for Bedazzled T-shirts our first season was off the charts at $15.00 per shirt. Using our 45 percent markup as a rule of thumb, we would have had to sell our T-shirts for $21.75 in order for us to protect a 30 percent gross margin. We did sell some to a few high-end boutiques, but we didn't sell lots of them. In our second season, we chose to simplify the design in order to lower the COGS. We did this by screen-printing equally beautiful but much simpler designs. We cut screen-printing costs in half and reduced damages by 70 percent by changing suppliers, reducing COGS to less than $7.50 per shirt.

If the only information known is the COGS at $7.50 per unit, add 45 percent to get to the minimum selling price per unit to protect a minimum 30 percent gross margin. In our second season with Bedazzled, because we managed to reduce COGS so dramatically, we were able to sell our T-shirts for $10.87, which we rounded up to $11.00. That's almost half the price we were selling the T-shirts for our first season. And we sold thousands of more T-shirts as a result.

Whatever course you choose, don't sell the T-shirt for less than COGS plus 45 percent. That's the only way the business will generate enough gross margin to pay operating costs—fixed expenses, indirect variable expenses, and taxes—and generate positive profits.

Let's recite our mantra once again. Repeat after me: *Every product or service must have a gross margin of at least 30 percent of net revenue or 45 percent above cost of goods sold.*

Fixed Expenses

The next line on the Net Income Statement reads "Fixed Expenses." **Fixed expenses** do not change with fluctuations in sales volume. Whether sales are strong, weak, or nonexistent, these expenses must be paid. These, as their name suggests, are going to stay the same no matter how many T-shirts are sold. Rent is an example of a fixed expense. Imagine that the business is renting some space and there's a month when the business doesn't generate much in sales. What would happen if you called the landlord and said, "Hey, Fred. We've had a tough February. Is it okay if we don't pay the rent this month?"

As Dr. Peter Wood, President of the National Association of Scholars, would say, that would go down "like a stinging nettles and wasabi sandwich." The landlord doesn't care. He just wants to get paid. If the business didn't sell any T-shirts that month, that's your problem. The rent bill is still due. That's a fixed expense.

Another pleasant way to think of fixed expenses is to imagine each one as a heavy noose around your neck that tightens if net revenue starts to falter. That's why the goal is to *keep fixed expenses as low as possible for as long as possible*. The lower the fixed expenses, the fewer T-shirts you need to sell to cover these expenses.

One of the smartest and most successful small business investors I ever met gave me this admonition: "Don't ever chase fixed overhead." He was essentially saying, don't take on fixed expenses that require the business to scramble to generate more sales to pay for them. *Grow sales faster than fixed expenses.* The time to take on more fixed expenses is when the orders are in your hands and the business has to scramble to get the orders out. The best managers take on fixed expenses when the marketplace has already voted for their products by purchasing them. Let net revenue and gross margin drive the right level of expenses, not the other way around. This is the Holy Grail of small business management.

Variable Expenses

Variable expenses, the next category of expenses on the Net Income Statement, tend to vary based on sales volume. And that's why they're called "variable." But these are actually *indirect* variable expenses. (Remember, COGS is considered a *direct* variable expense, and as such—by convention—has its own line on the Net Income Statement.) As more T-shirts are sold, indirect variable expenses (sales commissions, marketing expenses, etc.) tend to climb. If fewer T-shirts are sold, variable expenses should be reduced.

Some variable expenses are a lot easier to control than fixed expenses. If the business has a soft month in sales, it's usually easier and faster to reduce variable expenses like advertising (a marketing expense) than fixed expenses like the rent or salaries. Rental leases are usually a mid- to long-term commitment and are difficult to terminate when net revenue goes down, while hiring a social-media guru, for example, is usually a short-term commitment and one you can cancel pretty easily. Direct mail or email campaigns are also examples of variable expenses that can be scaled back if revenues are soft.

Two variable expenses that deserve mention are depreciation and interest expense. You may or may not have these for the business you manage; just know what they are and how they work.

Depreciation
When you buy an expensive asset, or an asset that has a multi-year useful life, like a piece of equipment or even a building, our friends at the Internal Revenue Service have rules about how to count

these large purchases as business expenses. Typically, a portion of the total expense is deducted each year according to a schedule over the useful life of that asset until the total original cost is accounted for. That partial expense recognition is called **depreciation** and you'll often see that as a budget line on a Net Income Statement. This is not a cash expense, but a true cost of doing business. At some point, the business will have to renovate the building and replace that worn-out equipment or computer.

Why do we need to depreciate these expenses instead of just showing the total cost on the Net Income Statement the year it was purchased? Because you don't "use up" an asset like a computer in one year, so you don't expense the entire cost of the computer on your Net Income Statement in the year you purchased it. It typically has a useful three-year life. There are conventions for depreciating various kinds of assets. Depreciation expense can be the same or vary year to year and can show up as either a fixed or variable expense, depending on the depreciation method determined by the accountant. It helps reduce the tax expense for the business in the years depreciation is recognized because it reduces earnings before taxes and therefore the amount of taxes a company pays. It shows up as a fixed expense year after year until the underlying long-term asset is fully depreciated. Paying less in taxes also helps to conserve cash, a very useful thing when cash is tight. We'll get into that in Chapter 5 when we introduce you to the Cash Flow Statement. The accountant will know all this and more. Don't sweat it. Just know that depreciation exists and it shows up as either a fixed or variable expense before earnings and before taxes are calculated. The next time you see this as a line item on a Net Income Statement, it won't be a stranger.

Interest Expense

The other variable expense that deserves mention is **interest expense**. If a loan or a credit line has been taken out for purchases made on behalf of the business, the cost of that short-term debt (paid within a year) is the interest expense paid. This interest expense shows up on the Net Income Statement on a line called—believe it or not—"Interest Expense."

Interest expense paid on long-term debt like a mortgage also gets accounted for on the Net Income Statement each month *as it gets paid.* (Don't be confused by the fact that these payments feel to you like fixed expenses; your accountant knows in which category to count it, and that's what's important to the IRS and your more savvy investors.) In summary, interest expenses on both short-term and long-term debt will show up on your Net Income Statement and will reduce operating income and profits. (We'll talk more about how and when to take on debt in Chapter 8.)

Earnings Before Taxes

If fixed and variable expenses are deducted from total gross margin, we're left with **earnings before taxes (EBT)**. The government makes a distinction before and after taxes, and so should you. Earnings before taxes are *not* profits. They are simply earnings from operations before taxes are paid to Uncle Sam, the state, and the municipality in which the business operates. There is a lot more to this subject, but for now, know that taxes are paid out of earnings before taxes.

Nothing affects how much profit a small business makes more than the tax line on the Net Income Statement. Anywhere from 40 percent to 50 percent of earnings is usually paid in taxes. For this reason, when taxes rise by even a few percentage points, it wipes out much of your profit (you probably know this already). Taxes are the last expense line on the Net Income Statement and they are typically one of the highest costs of doing business.

Small business managers often try to minimize EBT in order to minimize tax expense. That makes sense in the short term, but if the destiny of a business is to be sold, the selling price will be far lower than it would have been had the Net Income Statement shown higher operating profits over the years. Be sure to ask the accountant about this if selling the business is eventually the goal. There are several legitimate ways to calculate depreciation expense, for example, that will affect operating profit in both the short and long term. It all depends on what the endgame is. For me, I like to get a return on investment. If I'm investing years of effort into a company, it should be worth something at the end of all those years of sweat and toil.

Taxes

I promised you this book was not going to speak about tax laws and regulations and that we won't get into the weeds, but there are some basics you need to be aware of. You have accountants and lawyers to help wade through the details. Just know, in the United States a business will have to pay federal taxes. It may have to pay state taxes and, in some cases, it may also have to pay municipal or city taxes. As you can now see, tax rates have a profound influence on the size of the bottom line. It's the last expense line before net income. More than almost any other line item on the Net Income Statement, tax rates determine net income. When you hear about companies like Apple Computer relocating to Austin, Texas, or companies moving to Florida at the rate of 200 per month, last I heard, they are doing so because the tax rates are much more favorable for businesses there.

Net Income

Okay, let's review. After we've captured net revenue and deducted cost of goods sold (direct variable expenses), we're left with total gross margin. Then we deducted fixed expenses, indirect variable

expenses, and taxes. This leaves us with a final number: **net income**—also known as "net profit" or "the bottom line." These three terms all refer to exactly the same thing.

Businesses do not exist to break even or to show a loss for an extended period of time. If a business serves customers superbly, offers creative solutions, and takes on risk, it should be compensated for that. Positive net income is the key to staying in business. The profit mandate must be a priority if a business is to remain viable.

So let's see if Bedazzled, Inc. is generating positive net income. This month the business sold 1,000 T-shirts. Each T-shirt was sold for $15.00. It cost $5.00 to make each T-shirt. Fixed expenses this month were $2,000, and variable expenses were $3,000. Taxes are 50 percent of earnings. This is shown in Figure 2–1. How much profit did the business make this month? Drum roll, please:

BEDAZZLED

Monthly Net Income Statement

Net Revenue	**$15,000**	**100%**
Less: Cost of Goods Sold	($5,000)	33%
Equals: Gross Margin	**$10,000**	**66%**
Less: Fixed Costs	($2,000)	13%
Less: Variable Costs	($3,000)	20%
Equals: Earnings Before Taxes	**$5,000**	**33%**
Less: Taxes @ 50%	($2,500)	17%
Net Income	**$2,500**	**17%**

FIGURE 2–1

Woohoo! The business is profitable. It has generated a positive $2,500 in net income on the books at the end of this month. If net income is positive, the business is making money.

Just how profitable is it? That 17 percent on the right next to the net income number means that 17 cents of every dollar of net revenue is net profit. That doesn't seem like a lot of money, does it? Well, it's really not bad. If you managed the corner grocery store, for example, the bottom line would be more like two cents. That's right. For every dollar the neighborhood grocer takes in, it typically earns two cents—or even less sometimes. Next time you go food shopping, count your blessings that someone has the motivation to build a store, stock it, staff it, and maintain it so we can get our daily fix of coffee, eggs, and milk.

What if net income is negative? You guessed it. It would mean that you're losing money. Does this mean you'll soon be closing your doors? Not necessarily. You can weather a few lean periods and still stay in business. In fact, every business shows ups and downs in profit from month to month, because industries have different rhythms. If you're managing a retail store, the business will generate big sales in November and December, around the holidays. If you're managing a beach resort, the business makes most of its money from December through February, when snowbirds have had just about enough of shoveling snow. If you're managing a restaurant, it's best to be open on Saturdays, because that's when most customers are more likely to eat out, so Saturdays are high revenue days. In the strong net revenue months, profits will probably be positive. When net revenue is weak, monthly profit numbers might be negative due to the drag effect of fixed costs that, like rent, are always present whether a lot or a little is sold.

The goal is to show consistent profitability on a *quarterly basis*. The business can tolerate a lean month, but the goal is to adjust course and show a profit by the end of the quarter. If not, the business is heading for trouble. In the long term, a business can't continue to lose money and remain viable. If profits are negative for three months or more, something in the business is shaky and it needs to be fixed fast.

It's important to track net revenue and operating costs—indirect variable expenses—each month to identify where the problems are. If gross margin is not at or above 30 percent of net revenue, then look at what customers are buying, what price the business is charging, and what the cost of goods are. If the gross margin is fine but EBT is trending lower, then take a look at how much is being spent on fixed and variable expenses and find creative ways to drive them down. Ask how other businesses in your industry are managing those costs. Knowing the company's pattern of revenues and expenses also helps prepare for the lean months instead of being surprised by them. (Chapter 5 about the Cash Flow Statement will also help you do this.)

MANAGEMENT BENCHMARKS

Now that it's clear what the Net Income Statement is and what it measures, here are some benchmarks to help manage the business toward profitability month-to-month.

First, have the accountant or bookkeeper print a Net Income Statement of the business every month, typically after all sales and expenses for the month have been reconciled. Go over it line by line, just like we did in this chapter. Break it down until it makes sense to you. Don't be afraid to ask the accountant or bookkeeper to explain some of the numbers. (Accountants aren't perfect either and we didn't cover every possible type of expense here.)

Once you understand the numbers, now look at how the business is trending. Go back to Figure 2–1. Take a good look at the right-hand column that shows percentages. Everything is calculated off net revenue, which is shown as "100%," because that's the starting point.

Net revenue will always be the reference point for key ratios. Again, it's important to manage gross margin to be 30 percent or *higher* of total net revenue and COGS to be 70 percent of net revenue *or lower*. As a rule of thumb, fixed expenses should be managed to around 20 percent of net revenue and variable costs around the same level, around 20 percent, depending on the industry and how long the business has been operating

If the business can come close to hitting some of these benchmarks, that's terrific. Be aware that as net revenues rise, expenses will typically rise as well to scale the business to service more customers. In order to stay ahead, the key is to build revenues *faster* than expenses. Many new businesses, even those well funded, let expenses grow too quickly and burn out before revenues can cover those expenses.

Keep fixed expenses as low as possible until the business has a stable customer base that buys regularly. Keep running the business out of a basement, car, or living room—or on top of your head—as long as possible before you sign a lease to rent space. (There's a reason Apple Computer was started out of a garage in Cupertino, California.)

Only add products or services to the company's offering that generate at least 30 percent gross margin based on the price and the cost of making or delivering that product (COGS). Every product offered should *improve* gross margin, not degrade it. You *can't* make it up in volume. Please don't try.

In Chapter 3, we'll look at Net Income Statements from different kinds of businesses. The light bulb over your head will go off and you'll know what you need to change in any business to make it sing. Trust me. I've seen it happen in the real world thousands of times. Now it's your turn.

KEY TAKEAWAYS

▶ The Net Income Statement reveals whether the business is showing a profit or a loss. If your net income or bottom line is positive, the business is making money; negative, the business is losing money.

▶ The top line on the Net Income Statement is net revenue. That's where monthly sales are captured.

▶ The second line on the Net Income Statement is cost of goods sold (COGS). These are the direct costs to create a finished product that is saleable. It includes direct labor and direct materials.

▶ If the COGS is known, but selling price is not, remember that the business must be able to sell the item for COGS plus a 45 percent premium to be worth the while. If the marketplace won't pay that price, consider dropping that product from the lineup or changing its cost structure.

▶ Selling products at prices below COGS should be done only to flush out degrading inventory and only for a very brief time.

▶ The third line on the Net Income Statement is gross margin, or gross profit. It should equal at least 30 percent of net revenue in order to generate enough gross profit to pay fixed and variable expenses.

▶ Adequate gross margin is key to running a profitable business and must be measured every month. The Net Income Statement is the only statement that tracks this.

▶ Fixed expenses don't change with sales volume. Keep these at a minimum and no more than 20 percent of net revenue each month.

▶ Variable expenses trend higher as the business sells to more customers. Keep these expenses to no more than 20 percent of net revenue to make sure they don't get out of control.

▶ Earnings before taxes is the subtotal after every cost except for taxes is deducted from net revenues. If EBT is at least 10 percent of net revenue, then net income will probably be in a healthy range.

▶ Taxes are paid out of earnings before taxes. A good rule of thumb is to manage net income so that it yields at least 5 percent of net revenue. That means for every dollar of sales, the business generates at least five cents in net profit, or bottom line.

▶ Delivering positive bottom line numbers consistently every quarter is the key to long-term success.

CHAPTER 3

Using Your Net Income Statement to Improve Profits

Driving with Your Eyes Open

Now that you understand what we learn from the monthly Net Income Statement—is the business making a profit or showing a loss—you have a framework for making decisions. The challenge is to use this information to manage your business so that you are maximizing profits while keeping a tight rein on costs.

Achieving greater profitability does not mean taking advantage of unsuspecting customers. It means delivering value to customers while being wise about how you invest your time, energy, and scarce resources (like cash) so you get the best return on investment. If a business is not delivering value for what it's charging, customers simply will not buy from the company. If a business delivers great products or services but can't stay profitable, however, it will only be a matter of time before the world no longer has access to those marvelous products and services. Profits are the evidence that customers like a business's products or services enough to spend hard-earned cash for them, *and* that management is doing a superb job of keeping expenses in line with revenue. Profits are one of the healthy vital signs of a sustainable, well-managed business.

DRIVING PROFITS FOR PRODUCT BUSINESSES

Let's climb back in our business management simulator and practice using our Net Income Statement to manage a business toward profitability. We'll start with one from a business that sells a tangible product: cupcakes. Is Cupcakes R Us making a profit? Take a look at the Net Income Statement shown in Figure 3–1 and decide for yourself. (Remember: a number in parentheses is a negative number.)

What's your verdict? If you said the business is losing money—$4,500 a month, to be exact—you'd be correct. Clearly, something has to change if Cupcakes R Us is to stay in business. Let's do the diagnostics on this Net Income Statement to see why they're losing money. The first thing I zero in on is to see if gross margin meets our 30 percent of net revenue hurdle rate. If it doesn't, we need to find ways to increase it if we want to stay in business.

How to Increase Gross Margin

The challenge for Cupcakes R Us is that the gross margin is too low to be able to pay all the expenses to operate the business. The only way to turn this negative net income into a positive net income is to find ways to increase gross margin. Here are some ways to accomplish that.

Cupcakes R Us
Month of January

Net Revenue	**$4,500**	**100%**
Cost of Goods Sold	**($3,500)**	**78%**
Total Gross Margin	**$1,000**	**22%**
Fixed Expenses:		
Rent	($1,500)	33%
Variable Expenses:		
Marketing	($1,000)	
Utilities	($150)	
Phone	($100)	
Insurance	($150)	
Supplies	($1000)	
Part-time staff	($1000)	
Web support	($500)	
Bookkeeping	($100)	
Total Variable Expenses:	**$4,000)**	**88%**
Total Expenses	**($5,500)**	
Earnings Before Taxes	**($4,500)**	
Taxes	**000**	
Net Income	**($4,500)**	

FIGURE 3–1

Lower Cost of Goods Sold

The first benchmark we need to check is gross margin. If you re-member our mantra from the previous chapter, gross margin needs to be *at least* 30 percent of net revenue if a business is going to be profitable. Here, it is clocking in at 22 percent. And in order for gross margin to be at 30 percent or higher, COGS needs to be 70 percent or *lower*. As you can see, COGS is 78 percent of Cupcakes R Us's revenue. That means that for every dollar Cupcakes R Us makes in sales, $0.78 goes to pay for raw materials and labor to make the cupcakes. This is their unit cost. This number needs to get down to or under $0.70 to put gross margin in the safe zone. There are various strategies for achieving this, and the first one to investigate is whether Cupcakes R Us can lower its direct costs.

As I said in Chapter 2, very few small business managers know their fully loaded direct costs for labor and materials, and this ignorance is *not* bliss—it is driving blindfolded. To manage Cupcakes R Us, we need to know exactly what it costs in time and labor to measure, mix, and bake a batch of delicious cupcakes. We also need to know the cost of direct materials like the silky Belgian Chocolate, butter, flour, and sugar required to create these divine temptations. Finally, we need to know how these costs break down for each product on a per unit basis. Once we know the direct costs per unit, we need to look at our retail prices and make sure that they are marked up from that cost by about 45 percent. That will ensure that every product is helping us achieve a 30 percent gross margin. Remember, every product in the lineup needs to be making a 30 percent gross margin or it will degrade the overall gross margin.

Let's look at how direct costs break down for Cupcakes R Us. The bakery sells two kinds of cupcakes, chocolate and raspberry. As it happens, the raspberry cupcakes are more expensive to make than the chocolate cupcakes, and that cost rises in months (like January) when raspberries are not in season. So for January, our COGS breakdown per unit is as follows:

- Chocolate: $1.40 per unit

- Raspberry: $2.10 per unit

Now let's check these COGS against our retail prices. In January, chocolate cupcakes were priced at $2.00 each, and raspberry cupcakes were $2.50 each. We have to determine the gross margin (unit price minus unit cost) per unit, and then divide that gross margin by unit price to determine its percent of net revenue. For Cupcakes R Us, we're looking at the following numbers:

For chocolate:

$$\$2.00 \text{ (retail unit price)} - \$1.40 \text{ (COGS)}$$
$$= \$0.60 \text{ (gross margin)}$$

$0.60 divided by $2.00 equals 30% (whew!)

For raspberry:

$$\$2.50 \text{ (retail unit price)} - \$2.10 \text{ (COGS)}$$
$$= \$0.40 \text{ (gross gargin)}$$

$0.40 divided by $2.50 equals 16% (uh-oh!)

As you can see, gross margin on the chocolate cupcakes is just fine, but gross margin on the raspberry cupcakes is barely half of what it should be. Aha! Now we know exactly what is pulling the overall gross margin down to 22 percent of total net revenue.

The obvious next step is to see if we can fix the COGS on our raspberry cupcakes. First, it's nice to know the maximum COGS the business can afford. We know it needs to be *no more than* 70 percent of the retail price in order to get a 30 percent gross margin. So, if we keep our retail price of $2.50 per raspberry cupcake, then we need to bring maximum COGS down from $2.10 per unit to $1.75 per unit (2.50 times 0.70 equals 1.75). In other words, we need to see if we can produce and deliver each raspberry cupcake for about $0.35 less than we are currently paying. What can we do?

One solution is to offer raspberry cupcakes only at certain times during the year, when the raw ingredients are cheapest. In addition to lowering COGS, this creates a sense of urgency for customers to buy while they're still available. Other possible steps we can take include:

- Negotiating with suppliers for volume discounts.

- Re-engineering the product using different ingredients, construction, or materials.

- Finding low-cost collaboration. For example, if you are cooking out of your kitchen but need to expand, rent ovens or kitchens at commercial facilities instead of leasing an actual bakeshop.

- Finding new sources for raw materials.

Raise Prices

If we can't get our COGS down to 70 percent with these strategies, then we need to look at how feasible it is to raise our retail prices. Say that we can't lower the COGS on the raspberry cupcakes *at all*. How much would we need to raise the price to get a 30 percent gross margin? As I mentioned above, a general rule of thumb is to set the retail price by marking up our COGS by 45 percent.

We start by calculating the markup (we called it "the premium" in Chapter 2) and adding it to the unit cost.

2.10 times 0.45 equals 0.94.

$2.10 + 0.95 (we rounded up)
= $3.05 (new retail price per unit)

That new retail price is going to put our gross margin in a much healthier place. Price minus cost equals gross margin (GM), so:

$3.05 (new retail unit price) − $2.10 (COGS)
= $0.95 (GM)

$0.95 divided by $3.05 equals 31%
(and the Net Income Statement is healthy again!)

Alternatively, we can shoot for an exact 30 percent gross margin by establishing our current COGS as 70 percent (0.7) of the retail price (X). Here's how you figure that out:

$2.10 (COGS) ÷ 0.7 of retail price X, that is, COGS = 0.7X

$2.10 *divided by* 0.70 (70%) equals $3.00
(7 goes into 21 three times)

And voila! Our new retail price per unit is $3.00.

As you can see, if we can't lower our COGS, then we need to raise the price of the raspberry cupcakes by at least $0.50 per unit to get them generating a 30 percent gross margin. But will our customers spring for the extra fifty cents a cupcake?

Now, what if we are able to lower the unit COGS on our raspberry cupcakes some, but not enough to get them to 70 percent of retail price? Let's say that after negotiating with a new raspberry supplier, we shave $0.15 of direct costs off each of our cupcakes, bringing our COGS from $2.10 down to $1.95. Now we still need to raise our prices to reach a 30 percent gross margin, but we won't have to raise them as much. Using the COGS method, if we mark up $1.95 by 45 percent (1.95 times 1.45), we get a unit price of $2.83 (rounding up). Using the net revenue method—setting our unit cost of $1.95 as 70 percent of the retail price—we end up charging $2.79 per unit. With our new unit cost, we can sell the raspberry cupcake at between $2.79 and $2.82 apiece and make an adequate gross margin (that is, stay in business). As you can see, lowering costs and raising prices are strategies that work in tandem to reach your COGS and gross margin benchmarks.

Bundle Products
Another option is to bundle the low gross margin product with higher gross margin products in a minimum order. That way, customers need to buy several products in the line. In the Cupcake R

Us case, this means that if customers want raspberry cupcakes, we set it up so that they need to buy chocolate cupcakes too—as long as our COGS and prices are set so that the average gross margin on this bundle is 30 percent. Bundling products can prevent clients from "cherry picking," or only buying the lowest margin products, which can be the fast lane to low or negative profits.

Sell Volume, Not Just One-sies and Two-sies

Volume sales can be helpful because it's often possible to negotiate volume discounts on raw ingredients, driving down COGS in the process. Instead of selling one cupcake for $3.00, a single very large sale could be worth a hundred times that in revenue, with lower costs per unit. Unit prices will come down as well in this case, but it still may be easier to keep gross margin above 30 percent. Just make sure this is the case before investing in marketing to increase unit sales. For Cupcakes R Us, we would need to research our market and discover ways to sell large orders of cupcakes to customers.

What target audiences, times of the year, or times in a customer's life can we identify when customers are looking for volume? Parties? Weddings? Baby showers? Birthday parties? End of the year? New Year's celebrations? One high-volume order can be worth hundreds of dollars in sales revenue.

Drop the Low-Margin Raspberry Cupcake

Our last option to protect net income is to drop our low gross margin products from the line altogether. Sometimes dropping products that have a very low gross margin is a great way to send unprofitable customers to your competition. Ask customers their opinions. Will they pay more for a raspberry cupcake? Can you reduce the size of the raspberry cupcake for the same price? Let the customer help you make these kinds of decisions.

Eight Guidelines for Raising Prices While Preserving Sales

There are few variables on the Net Income Statement that will affect profits as much as pricing, because price drives revenue. Higher prices equals higher revenue—*as long as we don't lose sales in the process*. But raising prices equals raising heart rates for many small business owners. They think that if they raise prices customers will stop buying and run for the hills. But this is not necessarily true. Maintaining sales while raising prices is totally possible, as long as you are attentive to certain guidelines. The following are eight guidelines for raising prices in ways that will be accepted, rather than resisted, by customers.

Guideline #1: Check Out What Competitors Are Charging

Whenever I launch a new business, I become a mystery shopper and shop my competitors. I look at what the competition is charging for what they're delivering. Are they using better-quality ingredients or materials in their products? Do they have the same variety I do? Is their customer service fantastic or awful? Can I speak to a live human if I have a question? What's the total customer experience like? How are their customer reviews online? After I collect my data, I decide if their pricing is worth it.

I recommend that you check out at least five competitors in your market niche in order to judge if your prices are right. Incidentally, I've found that most small businesses tend to underprice rather than overprice their products.

And here's something you should remember about underpricing. It may seem counterintuitive, but one of the signs that a business's prices are too low is that its sales closure rate is too high. For example, a friend who owns an advertising company told me that his sales closure rate was 80 percent—eight out of ten people he presented to hired his firm. He was stunned when I told him that was a terrible closure rate. Why? He was closing all that business because his prices were too low. In that business, he'll know his pricing is competitive if he has a 25 percent closure rate. His pricing scheme meant he was serving too many clients at too low a gross margin. It was no wonder he could barely pay the operating expenses to run his company.

Guideline #2: How To Raise Prices and Remain Competitive
Say that we do some mystery shopping for Cupcakes R Us and discover that the cupcake competition is charging $3.75 for a raspberry cupcake that uses fillers, instead of the fresh berries that we use. Here we've been considering raising our prices to around $3.00, hoping that customers will buy them, and we find out that they're already buying an inferior product for far more. This tells us that we might be able raise our prices to $3.25 per cupcake or more and still be competitive enough to maintain our sales. If successful, our raspberry cupcakes would be delivering more than 30 percent in gross margin, which is our minimum goal. Granted, a

$0.75 jump in price may not be easy to pull off, but if our competition is already a lot more expensive, customers could be willing to compensate the business by paying more for a great product.

Guideline #3: Don't Raise Prices Across the Board
Raise prices on a select group of products—especially high-volume products with high perceived value, such as difficult-to-get or unique products. Customers will accept the new prices more readily. Keep other prices the same, at least for the short term. Give customers a chance to digest the price increase and give them an opportunity to get a break if they buy volume. Provide an incentive to continue to purchase from you instead of the competition.

Guideline #4: Raise Prices Incrementally and Not All at Once
Netflix was infamous for raising prices 60 percent in one shot. Customers were not happy and abandoned Netflix in droves. In general, a 10 to 12 percent increase won't raise the ire of most customers. Just make sure the business is not losing money on the most popular items. If the average of product prices can still deliver at least 30 percent gross margin, be satisfied.

Guideline #5: Give Customers Some Forewarning of Price Changes
Letting customers know about a price increase in advance allows them to prepare for it. Yes, this gives clients more time to shop the competition, so you need to know what the competition is charging before raising prices. It might also spike purchases now while prices are a bit lower. If you have particularly large and valued customers, take the time to call or meet with them before the formal correspondence about price changes goes out (and you may need to compromise a bit with the behemoths). Personal contact takes time, but it will earn the business a lot of credibility. It eases the pain of the message and helps protect core business relationships. It also treats customers like collaborators, not ATM machines. The golden rule applies to raising prices: Treat others as you'd like to be treated.

Guideline #6: When Publishing New Prices, Accuracy Matters
A valve company once sent all its customers a new price list in December. There was one big problem; the prices were incorrect. The actual prices were higher than the new price list indicated. Ouch. Check and double-check before the correspondence goes out.

Guideline #7: Timing Is Everything
The end of the year is usually a good time to announce a price increase for the New Year. Most business owners and individuals are accustomed to receiving news of price increases at this time. Insurance, health care, and utility companies often announce price increases at the end of the year. Give customers at least 30 days' notice before new prices tick up. Put up a clear and professional-looking sign in your retail premises. And if you sell to businesses and not just consumers, you should give them at least three months so they can factor the price increases into their next fiscal year budgets.

Guideline #8: Reinforce the Value Your Company Is Providing
It's not what clients pay for the product or service, it's what the business delivers that matters. Product prices and the way they're communicated should remind customers of how much those products or services contribute to their success. Price up, deliver professionally, and you'll be amazed at how a quality-conscious audience will be attracted to that offering.

Diversify Your Client Base

There's a bit more to be said about managing customers and understanding their impact on gross margin. In the same way that not every product contributes the same to your gross margin, not every customer does either. Every small business manager needs to look carefully at who is buying from the business, what specific products (or services) they're buying, and how much they're buying in relation to total revenue. This helps to identify which customers

have the most power to influence your revenues, and ultimately your profits.

Every customer or client is like a company in an investment portfolio. A healthy investment portfolio is designed so that one investment cannot jeopardize the return for the whole portfolio. Likewise, small business managers must learn to manage their clients so no one client can put a significant percentage of the company's revenue at risk.

I've used this kind of thinking in the real world and been amazed at how it's helped the businesses I've consulted with establish much more predictable revenue. I've also rarely seen this strategy emphasized in accounting texts. It's unbelievably powerful if you can implement it. A lot of smaller clients are a really good thing. It diversifies your revenue risk. Smaller clients can't demand big discounts. Your gross margin should be higher with smaller clients. So don't look down your nose at smaller clients—they pay the bills and keep the business afloat.

Incidentally, a diverse client base will make a business more attractive to investors, because they'll see that the business has manageable risk. For example, say you're an investor deciding to invest in one of two companies, Jane's Hardware or Joe's Hardware. Both companies sell very similar product lines, and both have 100 customers who buy from them regularly. However, the amount each customer buys varies dramatically between the two businesses:

Jane's Hardware	Joe's Hardware
Customer A = 90% of total revenue	Customer A = 10% of total revenue
Remaining customers = 10% total revenue	Remaining customers = 90% total revenue

What's the problem? Jane has one 900-pound gorilla customer. Every $9 out of $10 Jane's business generates in revenue comes from that one customer. That's great—as long as the customer continues to buy from her. What happens if that customer leaves? Jane's Hardware falls on hard times because she can't replace 90 percent of her revenue overnight. In fact, Jane will probably need to find *many* other clients to make up for the shortfall after that one big client leaves. Beating the bushes to find a lot of new revenue takes real time and effort. Additionally, Jane is probably carrying all kinds of operating costs to service Customer A, some of which are fixed expenses. When Customer A leaves, Jane is stuck with bills that keep piling up, while revenue has crashed faster than the NASDAQ market index.

Joe, on the other hand, has one customer who generates 10 percent of total revenue, and no other customers individually contributing more than 10 percent of the total revenue. He has a diversified client base. If a customer leaves Joe, his revenue will decrease, but his business won't be on life support the same way Jane's would be. He will still be able pay the bills with the revenue and gross margin generated from his remaining client base. He can recover faster. Losing one client won't sink net income into negative territory for Joe's Hardware. That's the beauty of diversifying your client base.

It's so important to realize that a large customer is not always profitable. In fact, large customers can sometimes be very costly. Anyone who has ever done business with a city, state, or local authority knows this. The customer has negotiating leverage on price, so they expect big discounts; they take a long time to pay; and they expect management to be more available than an obstetrician. The large client might also require a company to set up unique systems and processes to parallel their specifications in order to communicate to their organization. This could mean higher fixed overhead costs for the business.

If a high-maintenance customer insists on only buying the lowest margin products in the line, you need to have a meeting with the client to negotiate minimum orders and pricing. If that doesn't go well, maybe it's time to fire the client (nicely, of course) and send their low-margin business to the competition. It's always an option.

Don't Get Creamed

Here's another true story that will drive the client diversification point home. Imagine you manage a company that develops fantastic skin creams to stop the aging process—a veritable fountain of youth. A very large, upscale hotel chain catches wind of this product and places a ginormous order for it to sell in all its spas. That's a six-figure order for the business, the largest it has ever received. The champagne corks are flying all over the place celebrating this great victory. Now the company has to make the product and ship it to the spas, so the company borrows wads of cash from the bank to finance COGS, make the product, package it, and ship it out.

Two months later, management gets a fateful phone call from the buyer at the hotel chain saying the product did not sell. She wants to return *all* the unsold goods. Oh my. Guess who paid for the cost of goods to make the stuff in the first place? Guess who pays for the returns? Guess who probably has to sell all those goods at a scary discount well below COGS because face creams don't improve with age? If you answered "the business" to all those questions, you get an "A."

What's the moral of the story? One very large client can rattle your gross margin, cash flow, and profits to the core. Don't try to get the one big client and think life will be easier. It rarely works that way, especially when a business is small. The business takes on a lot more risk when it sells to large clients. It's also harder to control gross margin since big clients are price makers, not price takers. They tell you what they're willing to pay.

With a diversified client base, the revenue is much more predictable and the risk is spread out among equals. Build a solid revenue foundation for the business with predictable clients before trying to grow revenue fast with large ones. Yes, large-volume orders can help manage COGS, as I said in the discussion of Cupcakes R Us, but it's a balancing act.

A reasonable goal would be to have no one client representing more than 15 percent of revenue for the business (and less is even better). If that client leaves, the business has some resilience to replace that revenue with new clients. No matter how wonderful you are and how fabulous your products/services, sometimes a client will leave for greener pastures. Just don't get caught short when they do.

A Word on Marketing Expenses

Even though marketing is captured as a variable expense on the Net Income Statement, it should really be looked at as an investment that needs to show a measurable return in your net revenue and gross margin. What are your marketing dollars accomplishing? Is the business able to identify and close more relevant and profitable customers? Is the business able to close more profitable customers *faster* and more efficiently? In the case of online marketing, is the business attracting more relevant visitors who are investing more time on the website and signing up for special offers or newsletters?

For every dollar invested in any marketing activity, net revenue should gain five dollars. Why? Because typically, marketing budgets are around 20 percent of net revenue. Just keep it in mind. If a business is investing all kinds of money with social media and online marketing with no clear return, it's time to make a change.

DRIVING PROFITS FOR SERVICE BUSINESSES

Okay, let's move from talking about product businesses to service businesses. Reading the Net Income Statement for a service business can be a little more challenging than for a product business, because cost of goods sold in a service business looks different. You're not selling "stuff"—you're selling your time, labor, and expertise. This makes it difficult to keep score on whether your gross margin is where it should be. Since more than 75 percent of small businesses are service businesses, we need to spend some time on how to think about gross margin for a service business.

Your time has tremendous value. Every minute you squander is unique in the history of mankind, and you can never get it back again. Time is your only non-recoverable asset. In a service business, your entire success hinges on understanding this little-recognized fact. And there's no line on any of your financial statements that accounts for time. It's implied. It's also the greatest cost of doing business if you run a service business.

The Names Have Been Changed to Protect the Innocent

I want to give you two examples of service businesses managed by very smart and talented people who needed to recognize the true value of their time. Once they did, however, they were able to increase net income dramatically by focusing their efforts on activities that drove net revenue and gross margin, while maintaining great relationships with their customers. These turnaround stories will not only help drive this point home, but it might just change the future of the business you manage.

Example #1: Photography Studio

One of my clients owned a photography studio. We'll call it Fabulous Faces. She took three types of photographs: senior pictures, weddings, and family portraits. She worked 14 hours a day for 15 years, and never had any money in the bank at the end of the year.

We did a deep dive into her client base to see what percentage of clients were senior portraits, families, and weddings. All told, she had shot 70 senior portraits, 30 weddings, and 15 family portraits. Most photographs taken in the second quarter were for senior pictures, and in the third quarter they were for Christmas and holiday gifts.

I asked her the fateful question: "How long does it take you to shoot each type of photograph?" She said that she could shoot a senior portrait in two hours. A family portrait usually took three hours, because she had to calm down the screaming infant and help Grandma, who's moving a little slowly these days, get in position. In both cases, her clients could come to her, because she could shoot all types of portraits in her home or backyard, using natural lighting. She wasted no time in commuting or hauling her extensive photography and lighting equipment to another location. It was all set and ready to go in her studio.

Weddings were another matter altogether. She had to hire an assistant; break down her studio; load up the truck with lights, cameras, and backup equipment (since everything was being shot in real time and there was no opportunity for "oops"); and drive to the bride's house. The equipment had to be set up at the bride's house, photos taken, and then all that equipment got broken down again and loaded up in the truck to get to the wedding venue. There the equipment got set up again and more photos were taken. The whole backbreaking process repeated for a third time to get photos at the reception. By the end of the day, the photographer needed a hefty dose of Extra-Strength Something, because if it wasn't her aching legs from being on her feet for 12 hours, it was the headache from the mother-in-law who argued with her to "leave out that no-good Uncle Fred" from the photos.

After hearing what was involved, I asked our heroine why she shot weddings. She said, "I make good money on weddings." Hmmm. Let's see if that was true.

After I learned the hours required for each type of photograph, I asked what the average sale was for each photo shoot. Here is the breakdown:

Type of Photo	Hours Invested Per Client	Average Revenue Per Client	Compensation Per Hour
Senior Pictures	2 hrs.	$300	$150
Family Portraits	3 hrs.	$600	$200
Weddings	12 hrs.	$1,200	$10 after paying assistant a full day's wages and follow-up time

So how do you look at this? First, on a per-hour basis, after expenses, it's clear that family portraits were the most profitable. She made the most money for her time with them. For every wedding the photographer shot, not only did her family get lonely for her company on weekends, but she was also losing at least $190 in opportunity cost per hour. If she shot four family portraits in the same time it took her to shoot one wedding, the photographer would make $2,400—twice the $1,200 she made from a wedding. She also saved all the costs of paying her assistant. Next, if you added up all time spent processing photo files and working with the lab, framers, and the bride (who rarely makes up her mind fast) after the wedding, the photographer's original time investment more than quadrupled! The net result is that the photographer earned $10 per hour when she shot a wedding. She would have made more money if she had farmed herself out to shoot weddings for a large photography studio and charged $75 per hour after expenses, without all the follow-up headaches. Sometimes running a small business isn't the only way to make money.

What this photographer needed to do should be self-evident to you. First, she needed to shoot fewer weddings. If she loved the bride and wants to shoot the wedding out of the goodness of her heart, that's one thing. But if she thought she was shooting weddings to make more money, she was deluded. Her bank account was telling her that, but she couldn't see it.

Next, she needed to be keenly aware of how precious her time really was. If she could earn $3,000 ($2,400 plus cost of assistant) or more to shoot a wedding, then it was worth it. Granted, the market is limited at that price, but that's okay. So is her time.

Third, she should have been investing her marketing dollars to attract family and senior portrait clients. Since senior portraits are usually booked in the second quarter and family photographs in the third, these target audiences tend not to conflict. This is a beautiful thing. Senior portraits and family portraits compensate the photographer $150–$200 per hour.

Fourth, in theory, she could have worked half as hard by scheduling half as many sittings (saving half of her time), and taken home 50 percent more in revenue.

I wasn't positive, but I told this client that if she followed this prescription, by the end of the calendar year, she'd have $5,000 in the bank. I was wrong. She called me on December 15 and said she had $7,500 in the bank. We both cried. That had never happened. It changed her life.

Example #2: Interior Design Firm

An interior design business, ABC Design Corporation, had been selling expertise, creative ideas, and problem-solving capabilities for over 15 years. Unlike Cupcakes R Us, its services were not tangible, but they were mission critical for developers building large, commercial skyscrapers. ABC showed me a Net Income Statement that looked something like the one shown in Figure 3–2.

Obviously, ABC was profitable—its net income of $1,250 was positive. The company's bottom line was 5 percent of net revenue, or in this case, project revenue. That's actually pretty good. What ABC didn't realize was that they had big opportunities to increase net income that were easy to implement with big potential benefits. Scaling capacity and changing their price structure were two ways I recommended.

Scale Capacity to Grow Revenue

Again, in a service business, the largest part of the project-related expenses (which is the same as the COGS in a product-oriented business) is primarily the cost of direct labor, which comes down to time, skill/expertise, and effort. There may be some direct materials involved, but it's the labor customers are paying for. In the case of ABC, design projects broke down into different tasks requir-

ABC DESIGN CORPORATION
Month of April

Project Revenue:	**$25,000.00**
Project-Related Expenses (their "COGS")	($1,500.00)
Gross Margin on Projects:	**$23,500.00**
Fixed Expenses: Rent	($1,500.00)
Variable Expenses	
Advertising:	($1,000.00)
Salaries (Partners):	($12,000.00)
Insurances (health, disability):	($2,000.00)
Equipment:	($1,000.00)
Supplies:	($300.00)
Professional Fees (accounting, legal, IT):	($2,000.00)
Telephone:	($700.00)
Travel/Meals:	($500.00)
Subtotal Variable Expenses	**(19,500.00)**
Total Expenses	($21,000.00)
Operating Income Before Taxes	$2,500.00
Taxes	($1,250.00)
Net Income This Month	**$1,250.00**
	5% of Revenue

FIGURE 3–2

ing various levels of effort, skill, and time. It's important that the small business managers of service companies like this know exactly what specialized labor and time are required to deliver a particular service, for two reasons.

First, it allows them to price their hourly rates for each type of labor and make sure they're getting a 30 percent gross margin on each rate. Second, it allows them to identify strategies for completing projects more efficiently and managing a higher volume of projects. For example, most of ABC's design projects required drafting. While drafting is undoubtedly a skill most of the ABC partners possess, it was worth their while to hire drafters and reserve their time for aspects of projects that require their higher-level, higher-priced skills. Also, having more hands on deck to take care of the labor-intensive work allowed them to accept more profitable projects each week. I showed ABC that if they could afford to hire just one crackerjack drafter or designer to open up capacity for partners to accept more projects, they could improve project cycle time and achieve greater revenue and gross profit month after month.

Change Pricing Structure

If you look at ABC's direct project-related costs, you'll see that number is pretty small compared to project revenue. That's the cost of developing the designs and drafting the plans for the architects. When I first saw this Net Income Statement, my sense was that the costs captured there were not capturing their full costs. I guessed there was a lot of time the partners had invested in these projects that was just showing up as their salaries, instead of being allocated as direct labor against each project. I advised them that partners should know what their hourly rate should be, and then cost out each project based on hourly rate and the time it takes to complete the project. If the scope of the project changes, so should the final cost. If the project requires hard-to-find specialized knowledge, ABC should also charge a premium for that.

It's not obvious from this Net Income Statement, but when I asked Jared, one of the two partners, what he was charging for his time, it seemed very low. He verified this by calling ABC's top three customers to ask them why they hired the company instead of their competition. One response was, "You were the cheapest by far." Does this ring a bell? Remember the note on underpricing earlier in this chapter?

It was time to raise prices and maybe walk away from low-profit projects. It also meant that the partners needed to have a target compensation rate per hour to make any project worth accepting. ABC had not done that.

When we looked at each project, partner compensation varied dramatically. We decided that only high-margin projects would be accepted from then on. We also agreed that if the client wanted to change "just this one thing," ABC needed to estimate the additional time and cost that change would require. Then ABC should present the client a "change of scope" document, a formal letter telling the client how much these requested changes will cost and how they will affect deadlines. The client can then decide if they want to pay the additional fees for that change. If the client agrees, they sign and return the letter. This may seem cumbersome, but it's for the service provider's protection, just in case anyone gets amnesia by the time the invoice is sent.

In the past, ABC partners would make those changes *for free*, which drove their hourly compensation down through the floorboards! More hours with no additional compensation means less compensation per hour.

Now the client pays for any change, and decides which changes are important enough for them to pay for. It still means extra work for ABC, but at least they are compensated. If the client decides it's not worth it, ABC partners aren't working half the night for free.

Incidentally, ABC had another problem—they needed more office space. Their building on Fifth Avenue had space available, but that's expensive real estate in New York. Their fixed costs would skyrocket if they tried to expand there. So the partners decided they'd find loft space further west where they would not have to pay such high rent. There would be moving costs, which would be counted as a one-time variable expense, but the good news is that they would save on fixed expenses every month after that, to the tune of thousands of dollars a year. This, along with the other changes I helped them to make, gave ABC the potential to double their bottom line in six months or less. And they did!

Every Hour Is Not Created Equal

A few last words on how to calculate the value of your time, skill, and labor in a service business: Please do not price an hour of time as if every hour of the day has the same value. They do not. Different hours have different values. An hour of time at 2 P.M. does not have

the same value as one hour at 10 P.M. After 6 P.M. is personal time. If a client demands that a job get done on an accelerated timeframe, where the service provider must work after hours and sacrifice personal time to get the job done, the provider must charge for that.

One New Yorker who is a career counselor has a client who lives in Australia. This client is totally loyal to this counselor's wisdom. The most convenient time for the Australian client to Skype is at 10 P.M. The consultant was charging the same rate at 10 P.M. as she was at 2 P.M. and losing precious time with her family. I suggested she double her hourly rate after 6 P.M. The client could then choose to rearrange her schedule or compensate the service provider for the personal sacrifices required for after-hours counseling. The client now had considerable incentive to rearrange her schedule so the service provider was not inconvenienced.

Finally, if a service provider is a subject-matter expert, this increases the value of their time and labor, and the pricing structure should reflect that. One physician I met was a consultant and an expert in FDA-approval requirements. One of her clients complained that a project only took her several hours to complete and the price charged was too high. My response to the client's complaint was this: The client is paying for the doctor's specialized knowledge. In other words, the client is paying for the years of experience, not the hours to complete the task. Service providers need to know the value of their expertise, and communicate that effectively to clients.

* * *

Now you not only know now what a Net Income Statement is and how it works, you've seen a number of examples of how to improve the gross margin and bottom line for both product and service businesses. If it feels like we've covered a lot in this chapter, we have. This kind of thinking has turned around multimillion-dollar businesses, and can turn yours around as well. The best news is that it doesn't matter what a business sells. These strategies to improve a low gross margin and overall profitability apply to any and every business.

KEY TAKEAWAYS

Product Businesses

▶ Increasing price and reducing COGS will always increase gross margin on a per unit basis.

▶ It's important to check competitive pricing as a key benchmark to know if prices are right and demand for the product or service remains strong.

▶ If you know COGS and need to figure out what the retail price (revenue per unit) should be, add a 45 percent premium to COGS to protect a minimum 30 percent gross margin.

▶ Raising prices on key items, creating minimum order sizes, and reducing COGS through re-engineering the product or changing suppliers are all possible ways to improve gross margin.

▶ Diversifying the client base reduces revenue risks if a large client leaves for any reason. This is true for all types of businesses.

Service Businesses

▶ The cost of sales in businesses that provide services is the value of time and expertise.

▶ Remember, gross margin should be at least 30 percent of net revenue to build a profitable business even in service businesses. COGS in a service business is the cost of an hour of an expert's time or knowledge.

▶   Clients are paying for the years, not just the hours.

▶   It's critically important to track the number of person-hours invested in projects so there is a correlation between what is being charged and how much it costs in time to deliver the final product.

▶   If clients request changes to a project, a change of scope document should be filled out for approval that includes the increase of time and costs to the overall project. Both client and service provider's interests are considered.

▶   Focus on those clients who purchase the most profitable products or services from the business.

CHAPTER 4

The Breakeven Point

When Your Business Is Truly Self-Sustaining

If someone were to ask you, "How do you know if this business is profitable?" you would now be able to confidently go to the bottom line of the company's Net Income Statement to see whether it was positive or negative for the period under review. When that line is positive, it means net income is positive and the business is profitable. When that line is negative, it means the business is showing a loss. After three chapters, you are also familiar with all the variables that drive profits as well as with some sophisticated techniques of improving them to build and protect a positive net income. What may have seemed intimidating when you first picked up this book is now becoming intuitive. That's real progress!

Before I introduce the next gauge on your financial dashboard, the Cash Flow Statement (we get to it in Chapter 5), I thought it was important to introduce you to a key point in the life of a small business that most managers neglect: the **breakeven point**.

The point at which a business "breaks even" occurs when its net income is neither positive nor negative; rather, it is *zero*. At the breakeven point, a business's gains equal its losses. Net revenue is large enough to cover all fixed and variable expenses and the business has the potential to generate sustainable profits. This is why I call the breakeven point the "sleep at night" point. Obviously, we want to see positive net income, but most importantly, we want profits to be sustainable over time.

This chapter will show you how to look at the breakeven point. It will also give you additional ways to ensure that the profit potential of the business is protected in the long term. Every business has a different breakeven point because every business has different levels of expenses and revenue. That's why it's important to know what the breakeven point is for the business *you're* managing.

The good news is that all the data for determining the breakeven point comes directly from the net income statement. That's why we're discussing it here in Chapter 4, right after we've discussed the Net Income Statement and how it works in Chapters 2 and 3. This first gauge on your financial dashboard should feel like a comfortable old shoe by now.

But remember, a small business is like your car; it can operate at different speeds. If you want to manage the business toward *sustainable* profits that are generated efficiently, you need to pay close attention to this breakeven point. When a business reaches this point it means that it, like a growing adult, has become self-sustaining, at least in theory.

WHY THE BREAKEVEN POINT MATTERS

The breakeven point is the first triumph on the road to profitability. Reaching this point of self-sufficiency is a major feat for most small businesses. In the early stages of a small business, all expenses (total fixed and variable expenses) tend to be higher than net revenue.

Why? Because variable expenses, like building a website or promoting the business's products and services, can be significant and they pile up very fast, while net revenue comes in much more slowly—and unpredictably. It takes time for a business to build a reputation. It takes time for customers to experience the benefits of the business's unique products or services. It takes time for customers to buy this new product or service so the business can generate sales to grow net revenue. It takes time for customers to fall in love with a product or service and for their enthusiasm to spread to friends and colleagues so they become customers, too. And it takes time to measure the trend of net revenue so managers can begin to predict when new customers will purchase, what products or services they'll purchase, how much they will purchase, and how much gross margin will be generated from those purchases. These are the factors that drive net revenue and gross margin, which you learned in the last two chapters. (Is it time for another chorus of our mantra from Chapter 2? *Every product or service must have a gross margin of at least 30 percent of net revenue or 45 percent above cost of goods sold.*)

Building net revenue always takes longer than a small business manager expects. This is why I said in Chapter 2 that it's vital to keep a tight handle on all expenses in the start-up phase while net revenue is building.

Even if, month after month, the business continues to show negative net income, it's encouraging to see the *rate* of net revenue growth increasing. Eventually, as more customers buy, the business should become more efficient in servicing customers and net revenue will begin to grow at a faster rate than expenses. That's when net income turns positive and profits are being generated. That's what every business needs to stay viable.

When this dynamic occurs, you know the business is on the road to the breakeven point. If a business never achieves this point, it will never be profitable, no matter how much the world loves its products or services. *Until net revenue from sales is consistently higher than the total of both fixed and variable expenses, a business is not self-sustaining.*

HOW TO DISCOVER THE BREAKEVEN POINT

Let's look at an abbreviated example of a simple Net Income Statement for Joe's Auto Parts. Then I'll show you how these numbers look on a graph so you can see how to find the breakeven point. In order to figure out how many units must be sold to achieve the breakeven point, I will express net revenue, COGS, gross margin, and variable expenses on a per unit basis instead of showing totals as I did in the previous three chapters.

In this example, **net margin** is simply net revenue minus both direct variable expenses (COGS) and indirect variable expenses (operating costs) *per unit.* Or you can think of it as gross margin minus indirect variable expenses *per unit* (they are two ways of saying the same thing). Either way, this net margin per unit is what's left over to help cover all fixed expenses. That gets us one step closer to figuring out how many units need to be sold to reach the breakeven point.

We'll show *total* fixed expenses and not fixed expenses *per unit* because this number doesn't change if we sell one or a thousand units. Let's look at the first six lines of the Net Income Statement for John's Auto Parts, as shown in Figure 4–1.

Fixed Expenses Versus Units Sold

If a picture is worth a thousand words, let's use pictures to see what's really going on. First, let's understand what the graph in Figure 4–2 is measuring.

JOHN'S AUTO PARTS

Net Income Statement

Net revenue per unit =	$15.00
Less: **direct variable expense (COGS)** per unit =	($4.00)
Gross margin per unit =	$11.00
Less: **indirect variable expense** (operating expense) per unit =	($2.00)
Net margin per unit before **fixed expenses** =	$9.00
Total fixed expenses =	($1,500)

FIGURE 4–1

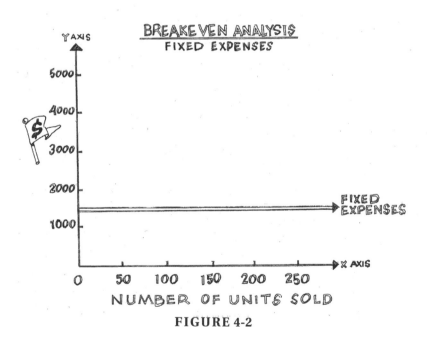

FIGURE 4-2

Along the bottom, on the horizontal line called the x-axis, you see the label "Number of Units Sold." As your eye moves to the right, the number of units sold gets larger. The vertical line, or y-axis, simply measures dollars, as the "$" label indicates. Here, these dollars represent fixed expenses, but they can represent anything measured in dollars: fixed and variable expenses, net revenue, or anything else. This comes in handy, as you will see.

I've graphed the fixed expense line alone in this figure. It's a flat, double line that illustrates that whether the business sells one unit or 200 units of anything in this example, fixed expense is the same. For John's Auto Parts, fixed expense is $1,500. Let's assume this fixed expense is rent. Until the lease terms change or the business moves, the fixed expense line will not change.

Fixed Expenses and Variable Expenses Versus Units Sold

But fixed expenses are not our only expenses; we need to consider the variable expenses as well. As you might remember from Chapter 2, there are two kinds of variable expenses: direct expenses (COGS—material and labor) and indirect expenses (sales commissions, Web support expenses, marketing expenses, etc.), which increase as the number of units sold increases. Because indirect variable expense increases with greater sales (more units sold), the variable expenses line will slope upward. In Figure 4–3, we added the variable expenses line (the dotted one) to our graph of fixed expenses.

Notice the dotted variable expenses line begins at "0,$1500." This is because variable expenses are paid *over and above* fixed expenses.

Fixed Expenses, Variable Expenses, and Net Revenue Versus Units Sold

I mentioned that the y-axis measures dollars, and that anything that is measured in dollars can be graphed on this same quadrant. So we can add the net revenue for John's Auto Parts to this breakeven analysis and see what happens. We have done exactly that in Figure 4–4.

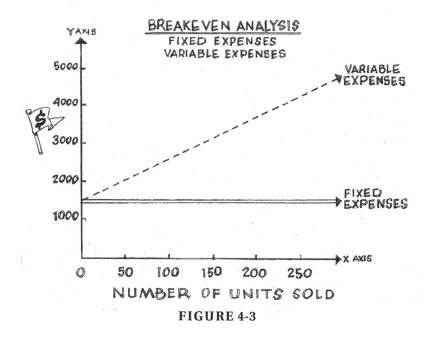

FIGURE 4-3

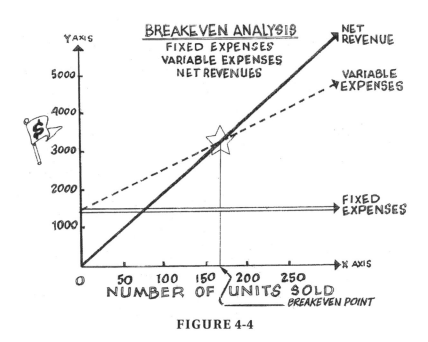

FIGURE 4-4

The thick, black, upward-sloping line on Figure 4–4 represents net revenue. This line traces how many dollars will be brought into the company by the sale of one, two, three . . . 200, 250 units (unit price times the number of units sold, remember?). Notice that the net revenue line starts at the point (0,0), because if John's doesn't sell anything, the number of units sold is zero, so net revenue is zero. As John's Auto Parts sells more units, both the number of units sold and net revenue increases. That is, both lines "head north." The challenge is to make sure that *fixed expenses and variable expenses don't grow faster than net revenue*, so that profit stays positive. That's the key to reaching the breakeven point as quickly as possible. If your expenses rise faster than your net revenue, the business is in trouble. If not this week or this month, then next month or next quarter.

Customer demand determines net revenue. Customers don't care if John's is spending too much or too little on things like rent or marketing. They do care if John's has the parts they need and if the service is strong or lousy. It's up to John to keep a tight handle on all the expenses needed to run the business. That's the key to reaching the breakeven point as quickly as possible. Keeping expenses low while growing net revenue—selling more—is the way to do this. This is not a book about selling more, however; this is a book about making smart business decisions, so I'll stick to that here.

Back to Figure 4–4. Notice the great big star at the heart of the graph. That's the breakeven point. That's the place where the number of units sold, and therefore net revenue, is high enough to cover both fixed expenses and variable expenses.

How to Figure Out Breakeven Unit Volume

You know that reaching the breakeven point is important, so wouldn't it also be helpful to know how many units a business has to sell to get to it? The number of units sold that corresponds to the breakeven point is called the **breakeven unit volume** (or "breakeven point volume" or "breakeven volume"). It refers to the number of units that must be sold to reach the breakeven point.

Going back to John's Auto Parts Net Income Statement, we see that the direct variable expenses ($4.00 worth of COGS) have already been paid from the net revenue, leaving him with $11.00, and that his indirect variable costs ($2.00 worth of operating expenses) have been deducted as well, leaving him with $9.00. This means that each unit sold generates $9.00 to cover the remaining expenses, his *fixed* expenses (the rent). This $9.00 is his net margin per unit (unit price minus direct and indirect unit costs). So let's figure out how many units John's needs to sell to cover the rent.

We can solve for the number of units we need to sell to cover this fixed expense of $1,500 per month. This will give us our breakeven unit volume per month. The equation is simple:

$$\text{Fixed Expenses} \div \text{Net Margin per Unit}$$
$$= \text{Breakeven Unit Volume}$$

$$\$1,500 \div \$9$$
$$= 167 \text{ units sold to reach breakeven point each month}$$

If you take another look at Figure 4–4, you'll see a thin line that drops vertically from the breakeven point star to the units sold line. It crosses the Number of Units Sold line at just around 167 units.

Profits Rise Above and Losses Grow Below the Breakeven Point

When I was running Bedazzled, I sweated over every single T-shirt we sold until we sold enough T-shirts to reach that breakeven point. I knew that until we did, Bedazzled would be showing a loss.

In Figure 4–5, you'll see two shaded areas, one above the breakeven point, the other below it. Look at the shading *above* the

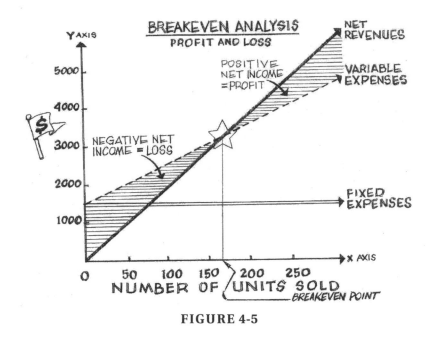

FIGURE 4-5

breakeven point star, the one labeled, "Positive Net Income = Profit." You can see as you trace the net revenue line higher (to the right), the business makes more money.

As the distance between the net revenue line and the dotted variable expense line gets wider above the breakeven point, the business becomes more profitable. That's when net revenue is growing faster than all expenses. That's what every business should strive for.

The Breakeven Unit Volume for Service Businesses

If you manage a service business, these figures apply to you as well. Instead of "Number of Units Sold" on the x-axis of the graph, imagine "Number of Hours Billed" instead. Conceptually, the breakeven point is exactly the same. The key question then becomes, "How many hours does the business need to bill in order to cover fixed and variable expenses?" or, "What is my breakeven unit volume in hours?"

The difference is that in service businesses, you're selling time and talent. Net revenue may be based on projects completed or hours worked, but at the end of the day it's important to know what an hour of time is worth, as I discussed in Chapter 3. The numbers of hours worked gets charted just like units sold. The more hours worked, the greater the net revenue should be. At least, that's how it should work. Know what you want to get paid per hour at each hour of the day based on your uniqueness and your competition's prices. If what you just read feels you've just read a foreign language, please reread Chapter 3.

Revenue Doesn't Just Grow; Sometimes It Shrinks

You can also trace the net revenue line down and to the left, below the breakeven point in Figure 4–5. The shaded area is labeled "Negative Net Income = Loss." Below the breakeven point, the dotted line is *above* the net revenue line. This shows that variable expenses are *higher* than net revenue. As you continue to trace the net revenue line even lower, there can be a point when both variable and fixed expenses are higher than net revenue. This situation is a real problem that needs addressing! No business is viable long term if it continues to show a loss. That's why we spent most of Chapter 3 giving you numerous strategies for decreasing various types of expenses and increasing net revenue and gross margin (remember those raspberry cupcakes?) so the business can start earning profit as quickly as possible.

Businesses can see that net revenue line slide back down below the breakeven point for many reasons. The following are reasons I've seen over the last 20 years, but trust me, there are many others.

- A decrease in customer demand due to a soft economy decreases units sold and, therefore, net revenue.

- Variable expenses rise, but net revenue doesn't rise as fast to cover these additional expenses. (For example, the business invests in an expensive online marketing program that costs a lot but delivers few new customers or no increase in net revenue from existing customers.)

- The sales force doesn't follow up diligently with prospective customers so net revenue potential is not realized while the business continues to pay the expense of the sales force's salaries and benefits.

- New competition comes into the market with large promotional budgets and steals customers who used to buy from the business you manage.

- New developments in technology make a product or service obsolete, so customers lose interest.

- The business might be too focused on selling old products, which reduces units sold and net revenue.

- The business's service support is poor, customer satisfaction suffers, and customers start buying from the competition, reducing units sold and net revenue.

IT TAKES TIME TO REACH THE BREAKEVEN POINT

It might seem easy to reach the breakeven point, but, in fact, it is pretty hard to do. Many small businesses never get there, which is one reason why the failure rate of small businesses is so high. Most people who manage small businesses think the problem is that they keep running out of money, but often the truth is that they are running out of time.

Reaching the breakeven point is a race against the clock. The goal is to reach breakeven as fast as possible, so that expenses don't sink the business before net revenue can catch up. Most small businesses do not reach their breakeven point for three to five years, if they ever do. The longer it takes, the higher the cumulative drag effect all expenses have on generating a positive net income.

You buy time for the business to build net revenue by working to keep all expenses as low as possible for as long as possible, especially in a weak economy. That's why we spent so much time on ways to reduce expenses and improve gross margin in previous chapters.

Keep Expenses Down to Reach the Breakeven Point More Quickly

By running a business out of a low-rent or no-rent location—someone's home or garage, for example—until it reaches the breakeven point, you can reduce fixed expenses. This will help the business reach predictable profits a lot faster.

If it's possible to rent equipment instead of buying it, do that. If it's possible to hire subcontractors rather than full-time employees, do that too. These tips can help reduce variable expenses. Is it inconvenient? Does it make life just a little more hectic? Yes to both.

In the early years at Microsoft Corporation, everyone—including Bill Gates—flew economy and ate inexpensive lunches to save money. Every opportunity Gates had to save a penny, he did—and look where he ended up! If it's good enough for Gates, it's good enough for small businesses to think this way too.

Larry Janesky, CEO of Basement Waterproofing Systems in Seymour, Connecticut, is a genius. He's also one of my heroes. He started this business when he was 17 years old and built it from nothing to over $100 million in sales with this kind of thinking. Now, he's taking this message to every contractor who will listen. In his book *The Highest Calling* (Relia-Serve Corporation, 2009), he admonishes small business managers to hold off buying that shiny new truck until all expenses are covered and net revenue is coming in at a predictable rate. He advises them to resist the temptation to rent larger, swanky office space until net revenue from the business is large enough, profitable enough, and predictable enough to pay for those fixed expense increases. Take it from the success stories; don't let optimism or your ego goad you into increasing any kind of expense too soon. Save money and you'll buy time.

Other Strategies to Reach the Breakeven Point More Quickly

The same strategies for raising gross margin and cutting expenses that we discussed in Chapter 3 should be used to race to the breakeven point. And here are a few more:

- Focus on profitable customers who are loyal to the business. Build the relationship with them and find ways to make the business more indispensable to them. This usually improves units sold and therefore increases net revenue.

- Focus sales efforts on products and services having a high gross margin.

- Renegotiate lease agreements, if you can, to drive down fixed expenses. Or simply move to a cheaper part of town.

- Convert full-time staff to part-time staff to save on benefits costs, reducing variable expenses. This may not be an easy option, but trust me, bankruptcy is far more difficult.

Experienced business managers keep a keen eye on that breakeven point and stop at nothing to make sure the business gets there as quickly as possible.

The time it takes to reach the breakeven point is also affected by the economy. In a strong economy, it's much easier to get there. Employment is strong, and consumers and businesses are buying more products and services because there's more discretionary income available as the economy expands. In weak economies, it takes longer to reach that breakeven point because unemployment is high and it's more challenging to find customers who are willing and able to buy products and services. It may cost the same to open a business in a weak economy, but that net revenue line will be flatter and take longer to cross the variable expense line to get to the breakeven point.

MARKETING EXPENSES CAN HELP OR HINDER

Marketing doesn't come cheap. You're not mimeographing a flyer on a borrowed machine in the church basement and paying your daughter $2.00 an hour to put them under windshield wipers. Marketing expenses can be a serious drain on the business's cash (you will learn about this in some detail in Chapter 5). Your goal is to make marketing expenses more efficient as you sell more units. In other words, it should take less marketing expense to find new customers.

Getting a Return on Investment
for Marketing Expenses Is Key

Marketing should be viewed as an investment, even though it's captured as a variable expense on the Net Income Statement. The difference between an investment and an expense is important. When you make an investment in your personal life, you expect to get a return on that investment, a premium over and above the value of your original investment for taking a risk. It's no different with a business.

If the business spends a dollar on a campaign to promote its website and that campaign delivers $5.00 in new net revenue, the business got a return on its investment. If the business invests in a social media campaign and sees no improvement in traffic to its site or additional net revenue, that campaign becomes a **sunk cost**—an expense that has yielded no benefit and can never be recovered. If the business builds up a lot of sunk costs, the breakeven point will likely be harder to reach and will have to sell many more units to cover these additional expenses. Faster growth in expenses of any kind without a corresponding increase in net revenue guarantees the likelihood the business will slip below the breakeven point and show a loss.

Many small business managers fall into the trap of hiring online marketers and end up with very little return for this variable expense. (I felt the sting of this when I was launching Best Small Biz Help.com.) If the business hires professional marketers to promote products or services online or offline, make sure that expense is quickly providing a return on investment for the business. To do this, you must be clear on the measures of success.

Establish Benchmarks for Performance to Get a Return on Marketing Expenses

When you invest in a marketing campaign, you should know how to measure what improved as a result. What are reasonable expectations for number of new prospects attracted to the business, or number of new visitors signed up for the newsletter? In what period of time should this take place? These and other metrics should be discussed with your marketing professional before you sign a contract. If your resource doesn't want to discuss these measurements of success with you, that should raise a red flag. Move on and find a marketer who is willing to be accountable.

Be sure to compare those measures *before* and *after* the marketing campaign. You should see the needle start moving on those measures of success within *two weeks* of a campaign. If the campaign is working, invest more into it. If it isn't working after 60 days, reduce this variable expense or eliminate it altogether. This is one way to keep marketing expenses from getting out of control.

Here are some questions I ask to measure whether or not the cost of a marketing campaign was worth the expense:

- What improved after the marketing efforts began?

- Did the number of relevant visitors to the website increase?

- Did these visitors engage for a longer period of time than before these marketing efforts began?

- Was the business more efficient at finding new, qualified prospective customers?

- Did the quality of new customers improve?

- Did the campaign help build stronger, more credible relationships with existing customers?

- Did the business close more net revenue with higher average gross margin?

- Did the average net revenue from each sale increase (meaning existing customers are buying more)?

- Were there more repeat purchases as a result of the campaign?

Focus Marketing Efforts on High Gross Margin Products and Services

Along with controlling costs, you'll reach the breakeven point faster by focusing sales efforts on high gross margin products and services because they'll work harder to cover all expenses. If product A generates $5 in gross margin per unit and product B generates $10 in gross margin per unit, what product should the marketing efforts focus on? If you said Product B, that's the right answer and Chapter 2 really did make a difference in your thinking! Each sale of Product B throws off $10.00—twice the gross margin of Product A. Thus, the more of Product B that is sold, the faster the business reaches the breakeven point. Think of this another way; the more Product B is sold at a higher gross margin per unit, the fewer units have to be sold to reach the breakeven point.

This is why I believe you run a business on gross margin. You run it on net revenue *that generates at least a 30 percent gross margin.* Your Net Income Statement measures this, and now you know how to read it, where to look for it, and what to do if gross margin falls below 30 percent. This is no small triumph.

Implementing some or all of these suggestions won't necessarily be easy. But when the survival of the business is at stake, *no product or expense can be sacred* if it isn't contributing adequately to gross margin to help the business reach the breakeven point and beyond.

STAYING AT OR ABOVE YOUR BREAKEVEN POINT

Healthcare professionals ask, "Do you know your number?"— meaning your blood pressure. In business, the reference point that answers that question is the breakeven unit volume required to cover all the expenses to keep your business humming. This marks the spot where your business achieves a balance between net revenue coming in from customer purchases and expenses (including your hopefully handsome salary) going out to run the business.

Knowing your breakeven point helps you to appreciate the significance of your spending decisions. Knowing your breakeven unit volume, you'll ask, "If the business takes on one more dollar of expense, of either fixed or variable expense, how many more units of product or hours of services does it have to sell to cover those additional expenses?" You may decide not to take on any additional expense once you figure out how much harder you have to work to bring in new customer net revenue to cover it. When thinking about maintaining your health, the best strategy is to work on prevention. It's the same thing when you're running a small business—preventing falling net revenue, rather than trying to recover from it, is the best strategy.

High gross margin will always make it easier to cover expenses of any kind, which is why it is such an important part of your strategy to prevent falling below the breakeven point.

Another key prevention measure, discussed in Chapter 3, is protecting and stabilizing your net revenue by diversifying your customer base. If over 15 percent of net revenue is generated by one important customer and that customer decides to stop buying, losing that net revenue could plunge your business well below the breakeven point.

* * *

The breakeven point is like the big red arrow on a map at the mall. It shows you where the net revenues are relative to all expenses. The first place to go to figure out the breakeven point for a business is the Net Income Statement. It provides all the information you need to determine if your business is below, at, or above the breakeven point. If the Net Income Statement is showing a loss, a review of the breakeven unit volume will reveal how many more units need to be sold or how much expenses have to be cut to move profits into positive net income territory.

KEY TAKEAWAYS

▶ The breakeven point is the point at which net revenue from units sold is high enough to cover all fixed and variable expenses (that is, all expenses including COGS) and profits are zero.

▶ New and growing businesses must grow net revenue above the breakeven point to be viable.

▶ Existing businesses must prevent net revenue from falling below the breakeven point to maintain financial viability.

▶ Lowering all expenses and improving gross margin will always make it easier to reach the breakeven point.

▶ The lower your expenses and the higher your gross margin is, the faster your business will reach and exceed the breakeven point.

▶ Breakeven unit volume is the number of units sold the business needs to achieve to reach the breakeven point. The larger the gross margin per unit, the fewer units you need to sell to cover all expenses and reach beyond the breakeven point to profitability.

▶ Expenses must always grow at a slower rate than net revenue.

▶ Make sure profitable net revenue is coming in predictably before you increase any type of expense.

CHAPTER 5

Your Cash Flow Statement Is Speaking

Can You Hear It?

Just as a speedometer doesn't tell you everything you need to know about the condition of your car, the Net Income Statement doesn't give you the full picture of the condition of a business. Did you know a business can be showing a profit and still be going bankrupt? It's true. If you doubt me, just ask the character George Bailey in the Frank Capra movie *It's a Wonderful Life*.

Every Christmas, the networks dust off this classic and it never gets old. George Bailey, played by Jimmy Stewart, is manager of the Bailey Building and Loan. On Christmas Eve, he is devastated to discover that his Uncle Billy has lost an $8,000 cash deposit on his way to the bank. This was the entire cash position of the company, which in those years might as well have been $80 million. In one careless moment, the Building and Loan is about to close its doors, bankrupting almost everyone in town.

George becomes desperate. After vainly attempting to drown his woes at the local pub and then crashing his car into a tree, our hero staggers over to the suspension bridge in the freezing cold. Before he can jump to his demise, he hears a splash and a cry for help, and dives in to save a drowning man. While they dry off, the rescued man introduces himself as George's guardian angel, Clarence, and explains that he jumped into the river to save George from suicide.

"It's ridiculous of you to think of killing yourself for money!" Clarence scolds. "$8,000."

". . . How do you know that?" George asks.

"I told you, I'm your guardian angel," says Clarence, leaning into George's face. "I know everything about you . . . Let me help you."

"You don't happen to have 8,000 bucks on you?" George replies sarcastically.

"Oh no," scoffs Clarence. "We don't use money in heaven."

"Oh yeah, that's right. I keep forgetting," George retorts. "Comes in pretty handy down here, Bub!"

Yes, cash comes in pretty handy down here indeed. In this chapter, you'll learn why cold, hard cash matters so much. You'll also learn how to keep track of it, something most small business managers don't do until it's too late.

WHY CASH FLOW IS IMPORTANT

If you've ever given blood, you know what happens. You lie on a gurney, a needle is inserted into your vein, and your blood gets pumped out. But did you notice? The phlebotomist never pumps *all* the blood out of your body. Why? Because if they did, you would die.

Cash is to your business as blood is to your body. The definition of bankruptcy is running out of cash—not net revenue, not profits, but cash. Managing cash is mission critical to keeping a small business alive. Cash is like fuel in your car—it's what keeps your business running. Cash pays all the expenses. That's why we likened the Cash Flow Statement, which indicates the amount of cash you have in the bank, to the gas gauge on the financial dashboard in Chapter 1. If there's not enough cash to run the business, the business stops. Cold. Consequently, there is urgency in learning how to read your Cash Flow Statement—your gas gauge—so you can measure how much cash is left to run the business. By managing the cash position of the business carefully, you protect its future and prevent it from becoming dependent on creditors to remain solvent.

NET REVENUE AND CASH ARE NOT THE SAME THING

The Net Income Statement does not tell you what cash you have *available* to run your business. Contrary to what you may assume, the net revenue listed on your Net Income Statement is rarely the same as the cash balance in your bank account. When the business rings up a sale, the net revenue generated may or may not fully convert into cash. If you sell ice cream cones, you usually get paid right away. This chapter is not for those cash businesses. But if you invoice your customers, you can't make the mistake of assuming net revenue and cash are the same and that they accumulate at the same time. The cash payments from invoices outstanding may materialize at some point in the future, but not in the month they were booked. Or perhaps not all of net revenue will convert to cash because of discounts taken or customers who can't pay their bills. If net revenue does not convert to cash in time or at all, it could create a cash crisis that threatens the life of the business.

Why Net Revenue and Cash Can Differ

There are four basic reasons that could create discrepancies between net revenue and the cash in the bank account of the business. The first reason (in several scenarios) is that the discrepancy is a function of your payment terms and invoicing process:

- The business sells a product or service and ships the goods or provides the services on credit to the client. The client agrees to pay the bill at some point in the future. This sales transaction shows up as net revenue on the Net Income Statement. However, the customer still owes payment. Until that cash arrives, the business does not have the cash from that sales transaction. Not until the client pays the bill and the check clears does it show up on the Cash Flow Statement.

- There may be more than a 30-day lag between billing a client and the business getting paid in cash. As with the credit scenario above, the value of the invoice will be captured on the Net Income Statement as net revenue in one month, but the cash won't come into the business until payment is received the month after.

- Customers don't pay because the business hasn't sent the invoice yet. The client has no idea what it owes the business or it has conveniently forgotten it owes the business money. (I'm not kidding. This really happens.)

A second reason your net revenue and cash don't match hinges on discounting policies.

- Discounts can be taken for many reasons. For example, a customer receives an early payment discount that's not captured on the Net Income Statement's net revenue line, but that will be deducted when the bill is paid. (Net revenue is, in fact, sales revenues less any discounts, as we mentioned in Chapter 1. That's why it's "net.") So your net revenue will indicate $500, but your bank account will only receive $450.

- Customers negotiate a payment discount to the original invoice amount if they receive some damaged goods or unsatisfactory service. In this scenario, net revenue is again higher than the final payment in cash will be.

A third reason for the difference will come as no surprise to most of you; client behavior is the culprit. And how wondrous the myriad ways . . .

- Customers pay with a check that bounces due to insufficient funds in their account.

- Customers delay payment or string out payment over a long period of time, possibly because they do not have sufficient cash to pay their bills. They want a free loan, essentially.

- Customers pay with an intermediary, like PayPal or a credit card. These third parties always take a percentage of the total purchase price for the payment convenience. The business receives most, but not all, of the value of the original invoice. If an online retailer, for example, charges $100 for an item, it might only receive $94 if PayPal or a credit card company (also called "intermediaries" or "third-party payers") is used to satisfy payment. The third-party payer gets the $6 difference as a commission or interchange fee.

  Why, you may wonder, does a business accept credit cards, or PayPal, if it won't receive full payment? There

are three basic reasons: first, each sale will be larger because people spend money more easily when they use a
credit card to pay for it (as you surmised); second, it gives
cash to the seller right away (useful for paying bills); and
third, the seller doesn't have to chase after the buyer for
payment, because that risk has been transferred to the
bank that approved the sale in the first place.

- A customer might place an order for goods or services,
then file for bankruptcy protection after the goods or
services are delivered (and the business has absorbed
the costs), but before payment is due. This is a disas-
trous state of affairs, and it happened to one of my small
business clients, a jewelry designer. He sold a $25,000
order to a well-known retailer that burned through all
its cash and declared bankruptcy. The designer had borrowed money to buy the gold, silver, and stones to fulfill
the order. He shipped the goods in good faith expecting
to get paid 30 days after shipment. Less than one month
later, the retailer went bankrupt. The designer never got
paid and was never able to get the shipment returned
either, because that inventory had become part of the
bankruptcy proceedings. If you guessed that the designer had to absorb the cost of manufacturing that inventory (the COGS, as we learned in Chapter 2) without
ever receiving the cash from the shipment, you're ready
for an advanced degree in small business management.
That's exactly what happened.

- To add insult to injury, if a customer *does* pay its bills to
the business and then files for bankruptcy within 90
days of that payment, under the "Preference Payment"
rules, the trustee overseeing the proceedings might seek
court intervention to return that cash payment to the

debtor's estate. In short, even after a business gets paid, the cash payment is not assured until that 90-day post-payment window has passed. I can't make this up. A great friend who is a partner in a law firm that specializes in credit and collections in New York City put me wise to this legal loophole.

The fourth and final reason that the monthly net revenue captured on your Net Income Statement and the amount of cash available in your bank account may differ involves the way the cost of capital equipment is captured on the Net Income Statement—that is, how the cost of depreciating assets is handled.

- Your business buys a new computer, paying cash up front for the full cost of a piece of equipment. Cash decreased the total value of the purchase right away, which will be reflected on the Cash Flow Statement. The Net Income Statement, however, will only expense or recognize a *portion* of that total cost in the form of *depreciation* expenses each year, until the total cost is realized over the useful life of the computer. Why? Because that computer has to be replaced within a few short years. The IRS requires the business to depreciate the value of that computer each year according to its useful life, recognizing that depreciation as a non-cash expense on the Net Income Statement.

It's important that you feel comfortable with the concept of depreciation, so let's take a look at it in greater detail. The discussion may seem familiar (I hope so), as I talked about it in Chapter 2. There, we were talking about the Net Income Statement and depreciation as a fixed or variable expense. Here, we are discussing how depreciation creates a discrepancy between net revenue and available cash. In the example above, annual depreciation reduces the value of the computer due to wear and tear and obsolescence. Therefore, the expense shown on the Net Income Statement and the cash outlay for that same piece of equipment will be different in the year it was purchased. The cash decreases by the full value of the computer purchase in the month it was purchased on the Cash Flow Statement. But net income will appear higher than it would be if the expense of the equipment were recognized all at once. The Net Income Statement will show only the depreciation expense for the computer in the year it was purchased. Just know, this is another reason why the annual cash flowing out of the business as captured on the Cash Flow Statement may be higher than expenses shown on the Net Income Statement.

As you can see, there are many conditions that create discrepancies between net revenue and real live cash in the company's coffers. As important as net revenue is, what determines whether or not your business can live to see another day has more to do with what your Cash Flow Statement says, which is how much cash is in the business's bank account at the end of the week, month, quarter, and year. (You should really be looking at this at the end of every week, by the way. Can't stress this enough.) If you manage to maintain a positive cash position by the end of each period, the business can stay alive through lean months, *even months when the Net Income Statement is showing a loss*. If you don't, however, your business will not survive.

What You Need to Know About Cash Basis and Accrual Basis Accounting

I should mention that the discrepancies between a business's Net Income Statement and Cash Flow Statement are also affected by whether it is using cash basis or accrual basis accounting to capture how and when sales are made and expenses are paid.

Most small businesses use **cash basis accounting** because it's simpler than accrual basis accounting. Cash basis accounting records when cash comes in from customer payments and when cash goes out to pay bills. Under this method, net revenue from sales does not get captured on the Net Income Statement until the client pays the invoice. Likewise, expenses do not get recorded on the Net Income Statement until the bills are paid. This method makes it easy to see the cash position of the business, and causes the Net Income Statement and Cash Flow Statement to track pretty closely.

The problem with cash basis accounting is that it does not provide the most accurate picture of the *timing* of when profits and cash are generated. First, it doesn't accurately capture the sales cycle—that is, when customers actually purchase a product or service. It only captures when customers pay their bills, which could be several weeks or months after the actual date of purchase. This can make the months in which customers pay their bills look far more profitable than they actually are. Second, cash basis accounting effectively blinds the business to upcoming transactions when cash will be coming into and going out of the business. For example, it doesn't show the cash that should be received from future client payments ("receivables"). Nor does it show cash that will be going out of the business to pay expenses against obligations the business already has ("payables"). I'll cover receivables and payables in greater depth in Chapter 7 when we go through the Balance Sheet in great detail. For now, just know that cash basis accounting doesn't capture the obligations *of* the business to pay bills or to the business of customers who owe it money. That is, if the cash event has not occurred yet, it's invisible. But these future cash events will have a profound effect on the amount of cash available to run the business. Cash basis accounting can blindside a small business manager unless he or she is careful.

For example, I did some consulting work for a dot.com years ago in NYC. When I asked one of the principals how many months the business could operate on their current cash reserves, he said,

"18 months." This meant the business could pay all its expenses for 18 months without having to earn one dollar of net revenue. I was impressed—that's a pretty strong cash position for a start-up company. Then I talked to the bookkeeper. Come to find out, the company had subcontracted dozens of programmers, who were working long, hard hours. They had not yet been paid, and their fees were rapidly racking up. The bookkeeper told me the company, in fact, had over $500,000 in unpaid expenses—an astronomically high number for a business that was not generating any net revenue, positive net income, or cash. It was clear the business only had three months, not 18 months, of cash to operate and to pay its expenses.

Their cash basis accounting system did not show the managers that the cash to pay the programmers had, in essence, already been spent even though the checks had not been written yet. Had the business been using *accrual basis accounting*, this growing aneurism of expenses would have shown up in the accounts payable section of the Balance Sheet (we cover the Balance Sheet in Chapter 7) and the cash would have been allocated accordingly.

Accrual basis accounting captures sales and expenses as they happen regardless of when the cash event occurs. Net revenue is booked when the goods are shipped out the door or invoices sent, not when payment is received. Similarly, expenses are booked when bills and invoices from suppliers or subcontractors are due, not when the business pays them. This tracks the timing of customer purchases and payments and the timing of when expenses are due more accurately. Accrual basis accounting solves the timing discrepancies of when a business's net revenue and expenses are captured and the cash is available to run the business. This is why the Net Income Statement and Cash Flow Statement will not track as closely with accrual basis accounting. Accrual basis accounting is the more conservative approach to keeping the books. There are no unhappy surprises with this method.

Accrual basis accounting provides a much clearer and comprehensive view of what the true cash position is for the business. (Your accountant will know all about this. Ask him or her which is being used.) For this reason, I recommend that every business, especially those that generate over $100,000 in net revenue each year, use accrual basis and not cash basis accounting, if possible. If the business you manage generates $5 million or more in net revenue, accrual basis accounting may be required by law. Ask your accountant to fill you in on this and any other legal stipulations. At least now, when you hear these terms, they will not be a mystery to you.

HOW THE CASH FLOW STATEMENT WORKS

By now you know that you can't take cash for granted. You have to manage your cash position, and it's actually quite simple. Your Cash Flow Statement, like your gas gauge, will tell you exactly how far the business can travel before it needs to fill up again. Everything on the Cash Flow Statement of the business only gets captured when *cash* changes hands; either payments are received or expenses are actually paid.

The Cash Flow Statement looks a lot like your checking account statement for your business. The business starts with a beginning balance of cash, we call that "**Beginning Cash**." Then cash comes into the business from various sources. That's "**Cash In**" (or "Cash Received"). Then the business uses up cash to pay expenses. That's "**Cash Out**" (or "Cash Expenses"). After all those inflows and outflows of cash are captured, and added and deducted from Beginning Cash, the business is left with "**Ending Cash**." That's pretty intuitive. Here's a simple example of a Cash Flow Statement by month for a fictitious photography business, One-Woman Photos:

	January	February	March
Beginning Cash	$10,000	$6,000	$5,000
Cash In	$3,000	$4,000	$10,000
Cash Out			
Rent Expense	($5,000)	($5,000)	($5,000)
Insurance Expense	($2,000)	000	000
Ending Cash	$6,000	$5,000	$10,000

Cash Received

Let's start with January and interpret what happened. This Cash Flow Statement tells us that One-Woman Photos began the year with $10,000 in the account for the business. The next line tells us that some cash payments came in to the business—$3,000 to be exact. Most likely, these were payments from invoices she sent out in November or December. The checks cleared and the photographer/business owner—we'll call her "Darla"—was able to deposit the cash into her account. That's a beautiful thing. That's Cash In.

Cash can come into the business for a variety of reasons, most likely the following:

1.   Clients pay their bills. Yippee!

2.   The business receives a refund or rebate of some kind. This is good, but it's usually a one-time event, so it's probably not enough to be a significant and predictable source of cash in the future.

3. The business invested some excess cash and that investment generated some interest, which was deposited in the business account. When the interest rates banks offer on savings accounts is low, this return on savings is negligible. When bank interest rates are high, as they were in the early 1980s, a return on cash savings might be significant.

As you can see, those first two items on the Cash Flow Statement are pretty straightforward. You now know the Beginning Cash balance and what cash came into the business in January.

Expenses

The next items on the Cash Flow Statement represent cash going out of the business to pay for expenses, or Cash Out. The photography shop has a monthly fixed expense of $5,000 for rent. It also has an insurance expense due in January—$2,000. This too is a fixed expense, but unlike rent, it is paid once annually, rather than monthly.

Take note that not all expenses are paid every month. Car insurance, for example, is usually paid semiannually (twice a year). Liability insurance (to protect people from mishaps on the premises of the business) is usually paid once a year. Thankfully, most of these less frequent expenses are fixed and predictable. Because fixed expenses like rent are stable month after month, you know you'll see the same numbers reflected on your Cash Flow Statement. Indirect variable expenses, as you know, tend to vary (hence the name—clever, those accountants) according to the volume of net revenue the business generates. Marketing expenses fall into this category, as do website expenses and employee salaries. These variable operating expenses are a bit more difficult to predict, but some of them can be controlled. For instance, a small business manager can choose to hire employees or to invest in an online marketing campaign or not.

Ending Cash

The Cash Flow Statement captures the expenses paid out of the business in the month the checks are written—that is, when the cash event has occurred. After deducting expenses paid or Cash Out from Beginning Cash and adding payments received as Cash In, the final line of the Cash Flow Statement shows the Ending Cash balance for the month. In Darla's case, in the Cash Flow Statement for January, she started with $10,000; she received $3,000 in payments and paid expenses to the tune of $7,000—leaving her with a cash balance of $6,000 at the end of the month.

Notice that January's Ending Cash balance becomes the Beginning Cash balance for February. It makes sense, no? February started with $6,000. The business collected $4,000 in Cash In, paid out $5,000 in expenses or Cash Out, and showed a balance of $5,000 at the end of February.

Now, what would have happened if Darla had received no cash payments during the month of February?

February Cash Flow	
Starting Cash	$6,000
Cash In	000
Cash Out	$5,000
Ending Cash	$1,000

Starting cash for March would have been $1,000, not $5,000. Now imagine that the business started March with only $1,000 and then received no cash coming into the business in March, with $5,000 owed in expenses. That's a perfect example of a *cash crunch*. To cover expenses after just two months with no incoming cash, the business would either have to take out a loan or close its doors. Now you know why most small business managers have insomnia.

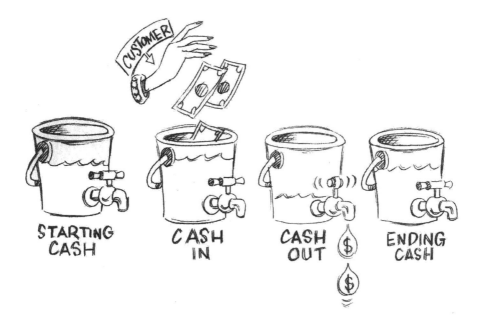

STARTING CASH   CASH IN   CASH OUT   ENDING CASH

BUDGETING CASH THE EASY WAY

So here's where the Cash Flow Statement becomes an incredibly valuable business management tool. Now that you know what the Cash Flow Statement is saying, you can take that information and start to forecast the cash flowing in and out of the business. Instead of driving blindly, not knowing how much cash is available at the end of each month to run the business, you can anticipate quarterly and yearly cash needs and manage them before a cash crunch hits. The Holy Grail of cash flow management is accurately predicting when cash flow will be tight and creating a budget that will cover the business's cash needs in those periods.

Don't be intimidated—building a cash flow budget is not difficult. At the end of each year, simply ask your accountant to print out the year-end Net Income Statement and Cash Flow Statement for you. Then use these as your baseline to predict cash flow for the year ahead. You can create a spreadsheet on the computer or write it down by hand. Put the 12 months of the year across the top, and put "Cash In" and "Cash Out" down the left column.

Start by listing your expenses, when they are due, and how much they are likely to be, based on the previous year's numbers. Rent, Web-hosting costs, salaries, and electricity should be pretty simple to predict (fixed expenses, a.k.a, your "monthly nut"). Legal and accounting expenses will probably be obvious too, assuming you have no outstanding audits or lawsuits. Plunk any non-monthly expenses, like insurance expenses, in the months you think they'll need to be paid.

Next, estimate the variable expenses you know will come. Phone expenses, freelance expenses, travel and entertainment, supplies, equipment repairs, marketing, and Web support—even the staff holiday party—are all typical variable expenses to include. Be sure to cover all the categories it takes to run the business, from soup to nuts. To estimate these expenses accurately, look at last year's expenses in those categories and consider whether or not they will be higher or lower in the coming year. Be conservative. If you think there are reasons they'll be more expensive (that's a no-brainer; they will be!) or that you'll have more of them (you may well!), round the estimate up.

Next comes the fun part: projecting cash coming into the business. This is a little more challenging, because it depends on how effective your sales efforts are, when clients pay their bills, how they pay their bills (are they taking discounts; are they using third-party payment providers), and, of course, if they pay you. Here are two good rules of thumb for predicting Cash In:

1. Assume at least a 30-day time lag between when sales are booked as net revenue on the Net Income Statement and when those sales convert to Cash In on your Cash Flow Statement.

2. Assume that only 90 percent of the revenue booked on your Net Income Statement will convert to Cash In,

whether due to intermediaries who take their cut or for other reasons, discussed earlier.

Your Net Income Statement can help you get a ballpark estimate of how next year's net revenue is likely to look each month. From there, you can predict that around 90 percent of that net revenue will convert to Cash In on your Cash Flow one month later. Write those predictions down in your cash flow budget.

For example, One-Woman Photos typically takes senior pictures in March for the yearbook trade. She invoices the clients when she gets the proofs back in April, and the clients pay in May or June. The revenue from these sales is captured on her April Net Income Statement when the invoices go out, but Darla books the cash in May or June when she receives and clears the checks from the clients. If Darla is trying to predict when she'll receive cash from her busy senior picture season, she has to account for that time lag. If she can reasonably estimate what her revenue for the coming April will look like, she can write down 90 percent of that number as Cash In for May or June of her cash flow budget.

Once you've predicted the expenses (Cash Out) and payments received (Cash In) for the business, you can identify when the Ending Cash is probably going to be dangerously low. These are what are affectionately referred to as "lean months."

For example, we saw that Darla's various insurance premiums (liability, health, theft, etc.) for the business come due in January, and it's a pretty hefty sum. In the photography business, there isn't a lot of net revenue generated from sales in January because customers are trying to digest Christmas expenses and are not in a buying mood. At the same time, there's a lot of cash going out to cover the large insurance premium. Darla knows she probably won't recoup that with cash coming in over the next month or two.

This is where she needs to use good judgment on how to pay expenses and to keep a tight control on cash until her Cash In picks up again in the spring and summer, which it usually does. For example, Darla may be able to negotiate a delay in the payment of other expenses or to break payments up into smaller monthly sums to help conserve cash in that lean quarter. Darla also needs to exercise some spending discipline and not buy that discounted backdrop in the first quarter of the year, even though it's tempting to take advantage of all those discounts. If her Ending Cash balance from December indicates she's got enough to pay for it without putting the business on life support, then fine.

As I said before, every business has lean months. There's seasonality to customer purchases. Most businesses have very hectic periods and slow periods. The hectic periods when net revenue is strong are the times to invest in the business. That's when the business generates the most sales and then, a month or two later, the most Cash In.

During the slow periods, it's wise to keep a super tight grip on expenses, not just on the size of expenses, but when you pay them. Don't pay anything you don't have to until the Cash In from customer payments starts to pick up. This will reduce the amount of borrowed capital (and accompanying interest expense) needed to run the business. It will also better manage the timing of the business's Cash In to Cash Out and help to avoid bankruptcy in the face of unanticipated expenses (the roof leaked, yikes!) or unanticipated drops in Cash In thanks to customers who have fallen on tough times.

CASH-BURNING TRAPS TO AVOID

Here are some common ways small businesses burn through cash and tromp down hard on the bankruptcy gas pedal. Although I only mention a handful, I could have written volumes on this topic alone.

Avoid Hiring Consultants Without Establishing Measures of Success

Dana, the developer of amazing proprietary software, made this mistake. Her business should be generating $20 million in net revenue per year. She should be working with every Fortune 500 company around the world. Instead, she is struggling to keep the lights on in the office. Dana hired a PR agency that was supposed to support sales efforts and generate net revenue. The PR agency kept saying it "just needed a few more months" to get the job done. They used that excuse for three years. At $1,000 per month, you can quickly calculate how much money she invested in this charade. The truth is, public relations efforts take time to show results, but a well-planned effort should begin to show results within three to six months.

Build in accountability! Determine in advance how you are going to measure the effectiveness of their efforts—and in what time frame. One measure of success could be how many people heard, read, or experienced your brand as a direct result of public relations promotions. Another measure of success could be growth in net revenue. If those metrics are not met after a reasonable period of time, fire the PR firm.

Avoid Hiring a Sales Rep with No Accountability

John, an architect, hired a fast-talking salesperson who managed to negotiate an annual fixed salary of $150,000 plus benefits—before generating one penny of net revenue. After being on the job for four years, the salesperson still hadn't even covered half the salary and benefit costs to the business. (Remember that the cost to hire a full-time employee is roughly double what their salary is.) So John's fully loaded cost to carry the salesperson's salary and benefits is, conservatively, $250,000 per year. Multiply that whopping quarter mil by four years, and you get a total expense to the business of $1 million. That's real money where I come from.

If you choose to hire a full-time salesperson or sales rep firm, be clear on how you will measure their effectiveness and in what time frame. Don't be afraid to ask when you can expect to see these results. And tie at least some portion of sales compensation to delivering those results. Everyone should be incentivized to do a great job.

Avoid Hiring Offshore Talent

Many small businesses hire resources halfway around the world because the hourly rates are so much less than they are in North America. But when you hire an offshore resource, you put the business into the hands of people in another time zone, outside your supervision, who speak a different language, have different cultural values, and may or may not be qualified to do the job you hired them for. What I have found is while the hourly rates are low, they can take twice as long to complete a task. The result is you'll burn through more cash than you expected and lose precious REM sleep too, thanks to those 3 A.M. conference calls.

Think twice, and then think again before you go this route. With all deference to Tim Ferris, entrepreneur and best-selling author, who is a big advocate of this, I've never been satisfied with the results. I took his advice and regretted it $1,500 and one month later. And yes, I consider sleep sacred.

Avoid Building a Website Too Advanced for You to Handle

Software options are changing everyday and it's daunting to know what is best for the business you manage. Techies like to use the coolest, newest software out there. Well, the software may be cool, but often it's unproven. As I learned the hard way, unproven software increases the risk of site crashes if you upload video, audio, or miss breakfast. When glitches occur—and they always do—you'll have to hire very expensive software programmers who need to build custom code to integrate this software with your mobile app or website and retrain your webmaster to update it. At $150 per hour, you'll see thousands fly out the door in the blink of an eyeball. This process has additional risk: you'll spend too much of your time managing the Web project and away from revenue-producing activities like calling customers.

Avoid Pursuing the "Magic Bullet" of Online Advertising and Social Media

Online advertising and social media programs can be very seductive, but they can also rack up expenses quickly and create major time drains if not managed effectively. Online marketing consultants who develop and run your online campaigns also represent risk, as does hiring an SEO (search engine optimization) expert. You pay these people big bucks, whether or not the site statistics improve and irrespective of any increase in your net revenue. You'll see a whopping increase in operating expense.

You can't avoid the Internet and social media, but you must be sure you know how to measure success with these programs—and know when to pull the plug if one or more of them are not delivering real value to the business.

There are other ways to burn through cash, of course, and I hope you avoid most of them.

Don't get me wrong—I'm not telling you never to hire consultants, off-shore talent, or hip Web designers. I'm telling you *to treat the cash you invest in these people like vital lifeblood.* For the sake of business survival, these cash investments must generate sufficient Cash In back into the business at a timely rate. In a recession, every penny matters. So does risk of performance. Establish clear benchmarks for performance, and make sure your salary contracts do not bind you to keep paying low-performing employees. Keep the business's website simple and easy enough to handle. Test the market with content first, and wait till visitors are growing leaps and bounds before making the large cash investment to build the big kahuna site. Not everything you try out will be successful, but it's up to you as the small business manager to control the damage and protect the life of the business. As one very successful entrepreneur told me, the most successful small business managers are not the ones who never make a mistake; they are the ones who make their course corrections *sooner*. Be one of those.

KEY TAKEAWAYS

▶ Positive profits do not insulate the business from bankruptcy. Positive, consistent Cash In that is larger than Cash Out does.

▶ Net revenue booked in one month rarely converts into cash the same month.

▶ Net revenue and net income are measured by the Net Income Statement. Cash flow is measured by the Cash Flow Statement.

▶ Your Net Income Statement and Cash Flow Statement can present very different numbers for cash on hand, depending on when customers buy, when and how they pay their bills, and when the business pays *its* bills.

▶ Accrual basis accounting, not cash basis accounting, gives the small business manager a fuller and more accurate view of the cash position for a business. This accounting method captures both receivables and payable transactions that will occur in the future.

▶ The Cash Flow Statement is like the check register for a personal bank account. It measures Beginning Cash, Cash In (payments from customers), Cash Out (expenses paid), and Ending Cash.

▶ One month's Ending Cash becomes the following month's Beginning Cash position.

▶ It's important to view the Cash Flow Statement each week and at the end of each month, along with the Net Income Statement for the month.

▶ The process of budgeting in advance can help reveal what months Ending Cash will be high and what months it will be low during the year. This helps you make course corrections before a cash crunch can threaten the viability of the business.

▶ Assume a 30-day time lag from the time a customer purchases until the time the business receives payment.

▶ Assume that 10 percent of outstanding net revenue will never be converted into cash, whether because of the payment method used or because the customer is in a cash crunch. If the business converts all net revenue to Cash In, that's a blessing. It's also very rare.

▶ Keeping a tight rein on all expenses will always conserve cash. Conserving cash is the key to thriving in any economy. Now you know why.

CHAPTER 6

Managing Your Cash Flow

More Is Better

So now you know how to read your Cash Flow Statement and use it to build a cash flow budget. Hopefully you're convinced that conserving cash is vital to keeping your business alive, and that you need to closely manage the outflow of cash so every expense is serving to keep the business running rather than draining it of precious lifeblood.

The heart of cash flow management is the cash cycle. In most businesses, the cash cycle is based on **terms of payment** (which indicate the date full payment is due as well as under what conditions discounts can be taken) rather than a simple cash sale, and looks like this:

1. A sale is made.

2. The goods are shipped or the services are rendered.

3. As soon as the business has delivered, an invoice goes out with payment terms clearly stated.

4. Once the invoice is paid, the cash is deposited in the business's account.

5. Operating expenses can now be paid.

In a perfect world, this cycle works seamlessly. In the real world, problems can arise at every step. Thus, *every step must be managed*. A lot of people who run small businesses mistakenly think that the only way to improve cash flow is to influence Step #1 in this cycle: selling more. But as you saw in the last chapter, booking more sales revenue on your Net Income Statement does not automatically put more cash in your bank account. There are a myriad of factors that influence how, when, and if that revenue converts to cash, and all of those factors come into play *after* Step #1. Credit extension, invoicing policy, payable policy, dealing with customers, and negotiating with suppliers, banks, and internal staff are all management disciplines that have a direct impact on the cash cycle. If these are handled well, a business can achieve optimal cash flow from existing operations. Sustainable cash flow from operations reduces pressure to increase sales or borrow cash from outside sources. If the cash cycle is poorly managed, however, or, as is often the case, simply ignored, then the business is guaranteed to suffer from cash deficit.

In this chapter, you're going to learn some easy-to-implement strategies for streamlining your cash flow management and maximizing the amount of operating cash your business generates.

MANAGING YOUR CASH INFLOW

As you saw in the previous chapter, the primary reason cash comes into a business is that customers pay their bills. You also saw that most of the causes for a gap between revenue and cash have to do with how, when, or if customers pay their bills. Clearly, converting revenue to cash and improving cash flow has a lot to do with getting your customers to pay you, and especially with getting them to pay you *on time*.

Did you know that if a business doesn't get paid for its products or services within 30 days of delivery, the chances of ever seeing that money goes down dramatically? If those same invoices are still unpaid after 60 days, the likelihood that the clients will pay them plummets even further. Aged and unpaid invoices can threaten the life of the business, as products go out or services are completed with no cash coming in. (And yes, "aged" means exactly what you think: These invoices are getting older.)

Unfortunately, many small businesses end up on life support because their managers fall prey to the following myths about how the business gets paid:

Myth: *If the business delivered brilliantly for a client, then the client will automatically pay the bill.*

> **Truth:** If the business you manage does not have a payable policy that defines the terms of payment for every sale, and if that policy is not clearly communicated to the client, then it doesn't matter how brilliantly the business delivered for the client. You could still end up holding a wad of invoices that may or may not get paid.

Myth: *If the business delivers the final product for the customer, then the customer knows how much is owed on the project and will pay the bill promptly.*

> **Truth:** Only an invoice triggers the payment cycle. The client has no obligation to pay the bill until the invoice is received. If that invoice does not contain complete and accurate information, and if it is not sent to the client on a timely basis, then there is no guarantee that the client will pay the right amount at the right time. If

the invoice goes out days, weeks, or months after the project is finished, then guess when payment will be received? Days, weeks, or months later than it should be.

Most small businesses don't have a payable policy (or collections policy), and many of those that do struggle to communicate it effectively to staff, suppliers, and customers. Also, most small businesses, especially service businesses, don't invoice the same day they complete work for a client. That's the equivalent of committing cash flow *hari kari*. Customers are not going to look out for the health of your business's cash flow. That's your job.

Doing Due Diligence

Perhaps the most obvious way to protect your cash flow is to avoid doing business, whenever possible, with clients who are unlikely to pay their bills. Banks do this as a matter of procedure, as basic risk management. Banks will check the credit history of the business to determine if it has a good reputation for meeting its payment obligations. When a business offers payment terms for an order, it is effectively becoming a bank and extending a non-interest-bearing loan for the client. The business has to pay for cost of goods sold and all operating expenses until the client pays the bill. If a new corporate client asks you for payment terms, do the due diligence up front. Even if the client is a big name, check with its other suppliers to be sure the client pays its bills. If the client is a privately held company, ask for three references you can call to make sure they are credit-worthy. And actually go ahead and call them. Does it take time? Yes. Recovering from never-paid invoices also takes time. It's always worth it to do risk management up front.

When I had Bedazzled, Inc., we sold to hundreds of boutiques, most of which were owned by individuals doing business under a corporate name. One boutique in Florida initially purchased our

T-shirts on a cash-on-delivery (C.O.D.) basis. Over six months, we shipped four orders to them, each a little bigger than the last. For the first three orders, they had a check ready for us when the shipment arrived. Then, having established payment credibility, they requested 30-day payment terms for the fourth order. Guess what happened? They *never* paid us for that fourth, largest shipment.

Twenty years later, I can still get steamed over that unpaid invoice for one reason. It was my fault. After the fact, I checked with three other suppliers this guy did business with to see if it was just Bedazzled he had robbed. They all told me he never paid his bills. The irony is that the boutique owner had given me those references to check! He was betting I wouldn't call them, and he was right. I learned an expensive lesson I'll never forget. If I had only checked first, I would have saved the business thousands of dollars in lost cash. I thought I was too busy. Don't make the same mistake.

Here's another lesson I had to learn the hard way: Don't get too excited when a potential client leaves your competition to buy from your business. Find out why they left the other company. In some cases, they leave because they have a bad habit of not paying their bills and they're on the lookout for a new supplier that will give them . . . well, a free loan that never gets paid back.

Setting Your Payable Policy

Every business needs to have an established payable policy that defines the terms of payment for every sale. Customers need to know exactly when and how you expect them to pay you for services rendered or goods delivered. Clearly communicating these needs and expectations is essential to managing your cash flow risk.

Here are some key guidelines for developing and communicating an effective payable policy:

- *Know the payable policy in your industry.* Every industry has standard practices for payable policies, and most chambers of commerce can provide this information. Do customers typically pay in 30 days in your industry? Are they offered an early payment discount? Industry benchmarks vary and it's your job to know what they are so you can align your policy with those expectations.

- *Develop a payable policy that adjusts for variables such as order or project size and different types of clients.* Your accountant can help you craft your payable policy so it not only falls within industry standards, but also is tailored to the business's sales and clientele. Perhaps your payment terms should be different with large clients, frequent-purchase clients, or loyal long-term clients. You may also differentiate terms for large orders.

- *Develop a payable policy that requires an initial deposit and specific interim payments for multi-phase or multi-month projects.* If you're allotting time and resources to put a new project on the calendar, the client should show good faith by paying an upfront fee to demonstrate how serious it is. After that initial deposit, invoices should go out as the project reaches progressive milestones of completion as specified in the contract, so that the outgoing expense of delivering the service and incoming cash payments stay in sync. This reduces payment risk and opportunity cost. If the client decides to pull the project, which can happen as circumstances or players change, at least the business will have received some compensation for the work completed up to that date.

Here's a real-life story exemplifying this point, in painful spades. A designer I know spent six months working on a website. She invested hundreds of hours creating a wonderful, useful online asset for the client.

She billed the client after all her work was through and she never got paid for it. If she had at least tried to get a deposit against the contract, she would have gotten an inkling that the client wasn't serious about paying its bills before she did the work. Don't get caught in that trap; insist on that initial deposit.

- *Don't keep payable policies a secret!* Write your payable policy into all contracts for the business so that when a client signs, they know up front how and when they are expected to satisfy the invoices you send. Don't wait to communicate payment policies until after the client has purchased, the invoice is aged, and you're chasing around for payment.

- *Communicate your payable policy to all relevant parties, not just clients.* All your support staff and subcontractors need to know what your payable policy is. Your book-keeper should know. Your accountant should know. Any part-time or full-time staff member should know. That payable policy is part of your business identity.

- *Reinforce payable policies at every opportunity.* Print your payable policy in the footer or the body of your invoices. Everyone needs reminders that you take getting paid seriously. If you don't, why would clients take it seriously?

Designing Your Invoices

Nothing affects cash flow more directly than a business's invoicing policy. Here are some key guidelines for designing invoices that will actually make customers *happy* to hand over their cash for your amazing goods and services:

Rule #1: Get an Attitude!

Send invoices with confidence, not trepidation. If the business has delivered a great product or service to a client, the invoice merely indicates that this is an exchange of value—the business's skill for the client's money. Don't be afraid to charge the client, and don't wait to do it.

Rule #2: List the Benefits

An invoice is more than just a bill for services rendered; it's a strategic document that can connect the dots between the benefit the client received from the business and the price you're asking them to pay. Remember, customers don't hire you to do work; they hire you to deliver results. Those results are the end-benefit the client receives for all the experience, hard work, and problem solving you provide. First, make sure you clearly describe the benefit the customer received for the work covered by the invoice. Did the business develop a new landing page that generated more site traffic? Did you take 100 photographs capturing the joy of a new marriage? Did you repair 50 cubic feet of damaged flooring and improve the safety of a home entrance? Write the benefit directly on the invoice above the price you're asking them to pay.

Next, show the client the actual skill, labor, expertise, and sacrifice it took to get the job done (to achieve that benefit). If the number of staff hours is meaningful, be sure they are included on the invoice. This strategy of including the end-benefit the client receives as well as the effort required to complete the project provides a way to give value to the intangible.

By the time the customer gets to the price on the invoice, they know exactly what they're paying for. The business you manage will get paid faster and cash flow will improve.

Rule #3: Quantify the Benefits

A lot of creative types get insulted when customers balk at the price of their services. But that's just human nature. Customers need you to quantify the inputs required to deliver a wonderful outcome.

Savings are another huge benefit that customers love and need to see. Most people experience a certain satisfaction when they know they've gotten a great value for the price they've paid. That's what you want to give to your clients. If the project cost the customer $1,000 while saving them $10,000, the savings should get captured on the invoice every single time. If you completed the job early, indicate the number of days or weeks that were saved on the invoice. If the job was brought in under budget, indicate the difference between the original quote and final price. If you, as the project manager, decided to "donate" two hours of time to complete the client's project, indicate the two hours and the value they represent on the invoice, and cross out that cost and put "no-cost" or "0" cost. The client will see right away how much they saved.

I always include a line on an invoice reminding the client that I get the job done in a quarter of the time my competitors do. On a per-hour basis, I am well compensated. On a total-cost basis, the client gets the deal of the century. My invoices make that clear, and thus make my clients feel good about the money they've spent.

Rule #4: Personalize the Invoice

If you had a team of three people on the job, list their names. The customer then knows their job was not a commodity, but was shepherded by real people who cared about the outcome. Steve Jobs was a rabid believer in this concept—his original design team signed the *inside* of the first Apple Computers. It was pride of ownership.

Invoices become a running record of the value the business delivered for every client—a testimony of what's been accomplished. Listing the benefits the client received is the key to differentiating your product or service from others. It will remind the client of what makes the business you manage different and more professional than that of your peers. It also supports a premium pricing

strategy, which is key to getting a solid return on investment for your time. Invoices help to build the reputation of the business.

Invoicing Strategy

Now that you know how to approach designing your invoices, let's talk about how and when to deliver them.

Same-Day Invoicing
Service businesses should invoice the client the *same day* they complete work for the client. It's astounding to me how few service businesses follow this simple rule. Do not let the sun go down on the day you complete a project without invoicing the client!

I hired a Web developer to work on Best Small Biz Help.com who didn't invoice me for nine months. That's thousands of dollars of work his business should have received but didn't. It's important for me to keep my payables up to date because it's my reputation on the line. As a client, I couldn't pay the bill without knowing how much I owed! I called him five times to ask for an invoice. That's a new twist—the client calls multiple times to ask for a bill. When I asked my rep who works with the firm what was going on, she said, "I hear this from many clients." If you wanted to commit cash-flow suicide, this is the way to do it.

Learn the lesson. When you communicate your payable policy at the beginning of a project, let your client know that you will generate an invoice the same day the work is finished. That way there are no surprises. Then, as soon as the job is completed, send the invoice. *Do it.* The clock doesn't start until the invoice is sent. The sooner the invoice is sent, the faster the business will get paid.

Confirm Receipt of Invoice

When you send an invoice, always confirm that the client received it. If you send the invoice via email, send it with a confirmation request. It is too important to get lost. It also provides a paper trail in case someone leaves the company or tries to give any excuses for why your bill wasn't paid. If necessary, you can say, "You didn't receive the invoice? That's odd. I'm looking at the confirmation dated 11/11 saying you did." Facts are better than dreams, as Churchill said.

Smaller Invoices, More Often

The key to invoicing is to make it easy for customers to pay you. I know that sounds painfully obvious, but you'd be amazed at how few business managers really get this. What happens when you receive a very large bill, even though you knew it was coming? A knot forms in the pit of your stomach. It becomes a burden. Smaller bites always digest better, don't you agree?

For multi-thousand-dollar invoices, I recommend breaking them up into smaller dollar amounts and sending them out with greater frequency. That makes it a cinch for clients to pay you, which helps cash flow and reduces collections risk. It takes a little extra effort and forward planning, but that's not significant when you think about what the business has to gain as a result.

Executive Producer Jane Applegate of The Applegate Group once invited me to videotape some business tips for her small business audience. During the shoot, the cameraman told me that he had done a shoot for a big accounting firm. Someone at the firm told him that when they started billing their clients weekly instead of monthly, they got paid 30 percent faster. The cameraman took this advice and started billing his customers weekly. Instead of invoicing them $2,000 per month, he started billing them $500 per week—and he started getting paid in 10 days instead of 60. I wish we had captured *him* on camera! A minor change in invoicing can have a dramatic effect on cash flow.

Keep Track of Outstanding Bills

It's important to keep track of what invoices are outstanding (unpaid) and when payment is due according to your payable policy, and how long ("days outstanding") any overdue bill has been languishing in the client's To Be Paid pile. Every week you should know which invoices are due the following week. Most accounting software will keep track of the age of invoices with a click of a button. If you don't know how, ask your bookkeeper to pull the report to show aging invoices. This **aging invoices report** will show:

- All the invoices that haven't been paid yet.

- The due date for payment of each invoice and days outstanding.

- The amount due on each invoice.

- The client responsible for each invoice.

You can see how useful this report will be.

It's a good sign if the average number of days outstanding for your invoices is less than 30 days. It means someone's calling clients on a regular basis to make sure invoices get paid. The shorter the days outstanding, the faster the business converts invoices into cash payments. As you now know, an outstanding invoice older than 30 days is much less likely to get paid.

Call Clients as Payment Date Approaches

Successful business managers know they are in the collections business, whether they like it or not. They get on the phone to collect payment. They know that calling two days *before* a due date, not after it, will help to preserve client relationships. Why? When you call the client before payment is due, it's a happy call. It's a check-up call. You're giving the client the benefit of the doubt that they will pay the bill in good faith. You're just shepherding the process along. You want to do everything possible to make sure payments are processed efficiently. Ask if there is anything you can do to facilitate the payment process. Do they have all your information? Is it accurate? Does cutting a check take longer than doing a wire transfer? If there is required paperwork to have wire-transfer payments, offer to fill them out and return them the same day. You might get paid sooner.

Specifically, I recommend calling clients between Tuesday and Thursday. Mondays are usually too hectic and on Friday everyone's distracted before the weekend. Call either before or after lunch time. I like to call around 10 A.M. That gives someone a chance to wrestle the early-morning gremlins to the ground and is before their stomachs start growling for lunch. I promise—it's painless.

Build a Relationship with Susie

When you call a large client to check on your unpaid invoice, there's a good chance that you'll be talking to Susie. Who's Susie? She's the accounts payable clerk for your client. She's the one who cuts the checks at the end of the month. Susie is probably the most under-appreciated, underpaid person on planet Earth, yet she "holds the keys to the kingdom" for small businesses. She manages the cash position at the client. She is often the one determining who gets paid, how much they get paid, and when they get paid. There is a pecking order of who gets paid first at the client. They'll probably never tell you this, but it's real and you should know about it. Suppliers who provide goods and services that are unique or difficult to substitute always get first priority when it comes to getting paid. Since, as a small business manager, it's unlikely that you are the behemoth at the front of the line, the better your relationship with Susie, the more likely you are to get paid sooner rather than later.

Most small business managers spend a lot of time building relationships with the people who sign the purchase orders for their clients, but they never meet the people who ultimately sign the checks. Never forget that generating sales revenue is great, but getting paid is even greater. Find out who "Susie" is at each large client the business sells to. If possible, go meet her in person, shake her hand, and look her in the eye. When she sends you a check for payment, send her a handwritten "thank you" note by snail mail. *I'm not kidding*. Take the time. Why? Because no one but you appreciates how important Susie is to your business. Susie never, ever gets a thank-you note. She's completely taken for granted by everyone. You won't make that same mistake, and for this reason, you won't be a stranger to her when she sees your invoice. You might even consider taking her out for lunch on occasion. When you do, ask her, "So, how's it going?" You'll be amazed at what you'll learn.

Here's a true story about a lunch that paid for itself many, many times over. Years ago, I took the accounts payable clerk at a client out for lunch. He told me the client was about to go bankrupt—and about to default on paying my bill. The same day, I spoke to my lawyer and sent a formal correspondence to the client terminating our contract due to the fact that they had no means to support the remainder of our agreement. I respectfully ended my professional relationship with that client before the client ran out of money and was unable to pay future invoices. It was a close call. Thankfully, because I had already built a trust relationship with the accounts payable clerk, he was forthcoming and I was able to do some risk management before everything blew up. At least I would incur no further losses.

You *always* need to manage your relationship with the actual human being who is handling your invoices. This holds true even if the client is a municipality or government agency. The person who pays the bills is a real live person just like Susie, not some faceless bureaucrat. I once did a significant amount of work on a training program for a government-sponsored agency in my state. I sent the invoice on time, but after five months, I still hadn't been paid. Now, most government agencies march to a different drummer than the rest of the world when it comes to paying bills, so I knew it would take a while to get paid. The thing was, the colleague with whom I worked side by side on this program had submitted her invoice at the same time I did, and was paid within 30 days. It didn't make sense.

I called my contact at the agency we did the work for and, after a long runaround, managed to find out who the accounts payable clerk was. She happened to be located 500 miles away. When I called the clerk, I didn't nag, though I wasn't happy about having delivered a superb program and not getting paid within a reasonable time. I told her that I just wanted to know if my invoice was in the system and what might be holding up payment. Was all my payment information accurately put into the payment system? Was the invoice lost? Should I have included other information on the invoice? I also asked her if there was anything I could do to make her job easier. (When was the last time anyone asked you that question?)

In short, the accounts payable clerk was wonderful. I've forgotten her name, but not her kindness. I got paid within five business days.

In addition to building rapport with Susie, small business managers will do themselves a huge favor by understanding the world from her viewpoint.

Tailor Your Invoices to Susie's Sign-Off Privileges

Ask Susie about the limits of her sign-off privileges and keep your *invoices within those limits.* Commonly, Susie will have sign-off privileges for smaller invoices, typically under $5,000. If an invoice arrives that is larger than her sign-off privileges, she needs her boss or her boss's boss to give approval to cut the check. Why? It's good risk management at the client to make sure there's no fraud and their cash flow is protected. The problem for you is that when your large invoice has to be sent up the management chain to get the required sign-offs, the wheels slow *way* down. The larger the invoice, the more sign-offs are required to release the cash to pay it, and the greater will be the delay in receiving payment.

You should expect payment policies and cutoffs to become more restrictive when a business is operating in an economy that is not growing, because your clients are trying to manage their risk like everyone else is. If Susie had $5,000 sign-off privileges when the economy was booming, her sign-off privileges might fall to half of that when sales revenue drops and cash is tighter. This is perfectly normal—you just need to know how to anticipate and manage it. If you sent out $5,000 invoices before, you should start sending out $2,500 invoices, with greater frequency, if the total outstanding invoice is large. If the customer writes a big order, stagger-ship the order so you can stagger-invoice the client. Then, if the client has problems paying, you won't be out the entire value of the order. (I would have made a lot more money if I had followed this advice 15 years ago.)

Tailor Your Billing Cycle to Susie's Payment Cycle

Ask Susie what the payment cycle is at the client, and *send invoices to coincide with it*. Most companies pay bills every two weeks or every month on a certain date. Put those dates in your calendar or make your bookkeeper or accountant aware of them so you can send invoices in advance of each check-cutting date. Verify once a quarter that the process is still the same. If you send an invoice right after those cutoffs, you'll have to wait until the next check-cutting cycle to get paid. Waiting to get paid always costs money and squeezes cash flow.

MANAGING YOUR CASH OUTFLOW

In the last chapter, I emphasized how critical it is to conserve the lifeblood of your business by keeping a tight rein on business expenses, and I warned you about some cash-burning traps to avoid. Here I want to give you two more strategies for minimizing your cash outflow.

Control Subcontractor Fees

Most businesses will subcontract individuals or businesses for various services. Online marketing is a common example. Unfortunately, there are a lot of people out there promising to drive relevant traffic to a website or blog and delivering very little for a whole lot of money. How can you protect the business? Spread the risk. Hire resources that are eager to get paid on a performance basis, not just a flat-fee basis. This will encourage your search engine optimization expert to act as a collaborator who is just as invested in your success as you are. Structure the payout so the SEO expert gets paid *more* if site statistics improve dramatically than if you just paid him or her on a fixed cost basis. This way you spread your risk of non-performance and conserve cash at the same time.

If your small business website succeeds, you're happy to compensate the people who helped you get there. And if it doesn't, you're not left holding a large bill with nothing to show for it.

Another way to conserve cash is to limit the time your subcontractor invests in a project. I negotiated with one of my paid contributors to invest no more than two hours when developing an article for Best Small Biz Help.com. So I pay her a flat fee per article. If she can be more efficient and create a terrific article in less time, her hourly rate effectively goes up.

Ask Your Suppliers for a Discount

If the business you manage pays its bills on time and its checks never bounce, you have negotiating leverage with suppliers. Even if the business is a small customer to the supplier, a great payment history means you can ask your suppliers for either a discount or added value that could ultimately bring greater cash value to the business.

Review the current terms you have with each supplier. Usually, the terms are net 30 days, which means payment is due within 30 days after the order is placed. Ask for a 5 percent discount for payment on delivery or payment by cash if you pay the bill within 10 days. If the supplier balks, don't argue about the idea of a discount—argue about how large the discount should be! If you do this with every supplier, you'll be shocked at how much money you can save. The first task is to do your homework. Know if the supplier's competition is offering discounts for early payment. Have that knowledge so you can counter your supplier's offer with real data. Your suppliers will respect you and go the extra mile—especially in soft markets—but only if the business you manage pays its bills on time.

One of the most successful and well-respected entrepreneurs I know in New York City was a true collaborator with his suppliers, but he made sure his account was never taken for granted. Every year, he reviewed supplier contracts, combed the market for deals, and then asked for either a discount or extra value for his account. Sometimes it meant getting shipped a "baker's dozen" (13 units) of a supply while getting charged for only 12. Other suppliers offered free passes to trade shows or provided training programs for staff members.

Suppliers have great networks and knowledge, and few customers take advantage of the influence they can have. Perhaps a supplier's resident expert can come to the business you manage and hold a brief seminar on a topic that matters to you or your staff. Building your intellectual capital like this can add real value to the business. But if you never ask, you'll never receive.

Bank Fees and Charges

Don't let your bank overcharge you. Know what all the fees and charges are. These days, they can be significant. Investigate what the banking competition is charging, including small local banks, and be prepared to hop to a new resource after you close your books at year-end if the charges are climbing too fast. Small local banks often give better service, charge the same or lower fees, and are less likely to treat a small business poorly.

There are thousands of businesses who are paying debit and credit card fees they shouldn't be paying. I once had coffee with a bookkeeper who does credit card transaction audits for small businesses. His job is to find ways to reduce the expense of credit card purchases for his clients. He told me that if the business you manage accepts debit cards for purchases, there's a very high likelihood the bank is charging the same interchange fee on debit card transactions that it is on credit card transactions. This is inappropriate, because debit card purchases are very different from credit card purchases. Debit cards decrease cash that's been deposited in an account—just like writing a check. In contrast, a credit card account extends credit to the buyer to be able to make the purchase from the retailer. It's a short-term loan, and it carries a greater risk to the bank. The bank should not charge the same fee to debit cash that's already there that it charges when it extends credit to complete a transaction. The interchange rate for a debit card transaction should always be lower than for a credit card transaction.

If the small business you manage accepts both credit and debit cards to satisfy payment, check the statements from the acquiring bank and look at the rates the business is being charged for debit card purchases. Make sure your debit card transactions are *not* overcharging your business. Reduce those fees and increase your cash!

* * *

I don't know about you, but if I invest my soul in a project for a client, bill them, and then don't get paid for that work, it puts a real crimp in my attitude. I've paid for my learning curve on how to manage the cash cycle so that I can avoid that situation whenever possible. I promise you that the strategies you've learned in this chapter have the potential to dramatically improve your odds of getting fully paid, on time. These cash flow tips may not seem terribly interesting—until you hear war stories about suppliers who lost their businesses and their home because clients never paid them. The stakes are very high. You're an insider now. No excuses.

KEY TAKEAWAYS

▶ Know what the payable policy standards are in your industry, and use these as a benchmark.

▶ Communicate payable policies for the business in writing on all contracts and invoices.

▶ Communicate payable policies to all staff, subcontractors, and suppliers up front so there are no surprises when cash has to change hands.

▶ Invoices are strategic documents. Use them to reinforce the value the customer received.

▶ If a project has multiple phases, receive a deposit up front and invoice the customer as project milestones are reached.

▶ When the business has delivered a product or service to clients, send out the invoices the same day. Don't wait.

▶ Get acknowledgments in writing that invoices have been received at the client.

▶ Call clients to collect on invoices that are approaching a 30-day age to ascertain when payment will occur and what you can do to expedite it.

▶ Meet Susie, the accounts payable clerk at the client. Develop an authentic appreciation for what she does. She'll help you manage your cash flow risk.

▶ Know the payment cycle at the client and send invoices to coordinate with that cycle.

▶ If the client owes the business a lot of money, generate more invoices with smaller values and greater frequency to avoid approval purgatory. The business will get paid faster.

▶ Ask for discounts for early payments and cash payments.

▶ Make sure your bank is not overcharging you.

CHAPTER **7**

What's Your Company Worth?

The Balance Sheet Holds the Secret

In Chapter 1 we introduced you to the three gauges on your financial dashboard: the Net Income Statement (speedometer), Cash Flow Statement (gas gauge), and Balance Sheet (oil pressure gauge). Now it's time to learn how the Balance Sheet indicates the overall health of a business.

If you ignore your oil pressure gauge, your engine can seize and your car will grind to a halt. If you ignore your Balance Sheet, so can the business.

If you attempt to continue to run the business without fixing the problems revealed on the Balance Sheet, you will be in pretty deep yoghurt. So it's a pretty good idea to learn what the Balance Sheet measures; primarily, it measures the relationship between the value of assets the business owns compared to the value of the liabilities the business owes.

While the Balance Sheet gets a fair amount of input from the Net Income Statement and the Cash Flow Statement, it also introduces new elements like receivables, payables, and owner's equity that you won't find measured by any other gauge on the financial dashboard. In this chapter, we'll define these terms, after first presenting the big picture.

WHAT THE BALANCE SHEET REVEALS

So you've been managing this business for a while and you're getting tired. The question is, what's it worth for all the time and effort and sacrifice put into it? Is the business only worth the breakup value of the computers, desks, equipment, and maybe the client list, or is there more to measuring its value? If so, what will help determine what the cumulative effects have been of all the decisions management has made since the business opened its doors? What gauge will we use?

The Balance Sheet holds the answer. It is a different animal than either the Net Income Statement or the Cash Flow Statement because it's more comprehensive. It is, as I said in the opening chapter, a snapshot of the health of the business at a point in time. The aggregate results of all the product decisions, pricing decisions, marketing and sales activities, cash flow management practices, expenses incurred, debt decisions, and investment decisions are captured on this one, clean tableau. Figure 7–1 presents a typical small business's Balance Sheet.

Any Balance Sheet, regardless of how complicated it looks on the surface, only has three sections to it: the assets, liabilities, and owner's equity of the business.

Assets are what the business owns and has title to. **Liabilities** are what the business owes or obligations it needs to pay either

A Typical Company
Balance Sheet

Assets		Liabilities	
Current Assets		**Current Liabilities**	
Cash	$$$$	Accounts Payable	$
Inventory	$$	Line of Credit	$
Accounts Receivables	$	Note Payable	$
Fixed Assets		**Long-Term Liabilities**	
Property, Plant,		Mortgages	$
Equipment	$$$	Bond	$
Less: Cumulative			
Depreciation	($)		
Total Assets	**$$$$$$$**	**Total Liabilities**	**$$$$$**
		Owner's Equity	
		Retained Earnings	$
		Equity Investments	$
		Total Liabilities	
		and Equity	**$$$$$$$**

FIGURE 7-1

now or in the future. The difference between the two is the **owner's equity** (net worth) that's been built up over time. Owner's equity can be positive or negative. If it's positive, that's a good thing. If it's negative, the little red light just went on and something needs to improve soon.

Think of the Balance Sheet as one of those old-time pan scales where the weight on one side—in this case, assets—has to be equal to the weight on the other—in this case, liabilities plus owner's equity. Here's how assets, liabilities, and owner's equity relate to each other in a simple equation. This equation will always be true, whether you're running General Motors or the corner convenience store.

$$\text{Assets} = \text{Liabilities} + \text{Owner's Equity}$$

In a perfect world, asset values are larger than liabilities, which means owner's equity is positive. If assets grow faster than liabilities, owner's equity also grows. This is what you want. It is one measure (but not the only measure) that the business you're managing is building equity value that could be sold at a future point in time.

Another way to think about the relationship between assets and liabilities is this: *Assets are what the business owns, liabilities are how the business paid for those assets.*

$$\text{Assets} - \text{Liabilities} = \text{Owner's Equity}$$

This second equation will give us the exact same result as the first one—and it provides a little more insight.

I like this form of the equation because you can really see what's going on. If we deduct what the business owes from what it owns, we have a clearer sense of whether our management decisions are growing or shrinking owner's equity.

Owner's equity is a derived number, which means we have to calculate it. It's the number remaining after you deduct the value of total liabilities from the value of total assets. The Balance Sheet for the business will capture what assets and liabilities are, and owner's equity is what's left over—or sometimes, unfortunately, what's in deficit. (Yes, it's possible to have negative owner's equity if liabilities are growing faster than assets. This is a condition that should be avoided like lead in household paint.)

Here's a personal example of how owner's equity and time interact. Happily, it is a positive one. After I graduated with my master's degree, I bought a condo in New York City for $125,000. (Yes, it was a long time ago.) I put a $25,000 deposit down and took out a mortgage loan from the bank for $100,000. My personal Balance Sheet showed the apartment as an asset that has a market value of $125,000. It also captured the mortgage loan as a liability for $100,000 against that asset. My owner's equity in that apartment was $25,000 at the closing. Over 10 years, apartments in New York became very valuable, so without my having to do anything, the apartment rose in value to $225,000. The asset value of the apartment rose by $100,000 and the owner's equity on my Balance Sheet rose $100,000, as you can see in Figure 7–2. And, in fact, it rose considerably more than that, because during those 10 years I had been "paying down" my liability (the $100,000 mortgage).

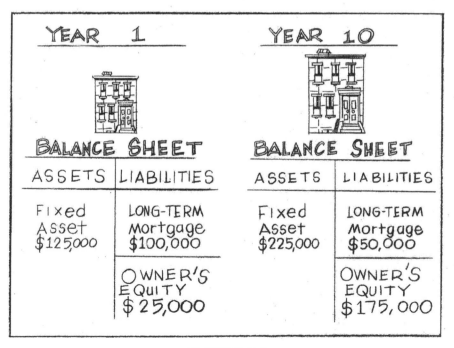

FIGURE 7-2

In short, the Balance Sheet captures the assets and liabilities in business as it does in our personal lives; it shows what the business has accumulated over the course of its life and ultimately measures the net worth of the business.

THE THREE SECTIONS OF THE BALANCE SHEET

As I did with the other two gauges on the financial dashboard, I'm going to take you through the Balance Sheet step by step. The beauty of the Balance Sheet is that it captures the cumulative results of running the business *over time*. It includes assets built, liabilities incurred, and equity that has grown through the day-to-day, month-after-month, faithful management of customer relationships, cash, and expenses. So let's go through the Balance Sheet, one section at a time.

Assets

Assets are cash or items that are convertible into cash. You'll always find these items on the left-hand side of the Balance Sheet.

Figure 7–3 shows the assets you might find on a Balance Sheet.

Assets come in two flavors and only two flavors: current assets and fixed assets.

Current Assets
Current assets include *cash* (not just the green wrinkly stuff sitting in a bank account, but also money market accounts, short-term CDs, and other "liquid" instruments), *accounts receivables* (money owed to the business), and *inventory* (the stock on the shelves and in the warehouse) that can be converted into cash within 12 months. You may have been a little surprised by my use of the word "liquid," but **liquidity** is an important concept that you must understand. It refers to how easy it is to sell an asset to convert it into cash. The more liquid an asset, the easier it is to sell. The difference

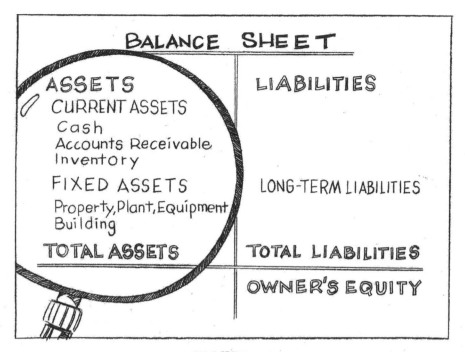

FIGURE 7-3

between a current and a fixed asset is that the current asset is more liquid and can be converted into cash within 12 months.

Cash, accounts receivables, and inventory are typically the three major line items you'll see under current assets on the Balance Sheet for businesses that sell products. For service businesses, you won't see a line item for inventory because you're selling time and expertise.

Cash Cash will always be the first line under current assets on any Balance Sheet. We like cash. The higher the cash levels, the better. Some accountants disagree, but since less cash is more frequently the problem than too much cash, I'm sticking to my guns.

The cash number on the Balance Sheet is fed from the Cash Flow Statement. It's an indicator of how long the business can pay its bills without additional outside sources of cash. It is also a function of how well the business is converting net revenue into cash through its collections activities and how well the business is managing expenses to conserve cash. You learned all about this in Chapters 3, 4, and 5. All roads lead to cash. As you now know, if a business sells products and services but doesn't collect on its invoices, cash withers to the point of bankrupting the company.

Accounts Receivable You will hear the term "**accounts receivables**" used interchangeably with the term "receivables" or "a receivable." Just know they're referring to the same type of current asset. If the plural is used, your accountant is talking about the *total* receivables for the business. If he or she talks about "a receivable," in all likelihood the reference is to a particular customer or entity that owes the business money on a particular invoice.

When the business makes a sale and ships merchandise or fulfills a service, unless the customer pays cash right away, a receivable is generated on that net revenue. More gibberish? This means "an invoice is generated for the sale made." You want the business to capture this and the Balance Sheet is the only place you'll find that receivables number. It means the customer owes the business money to satisfy its obligation as part of the bargain.

That receivable is considered a current asset for the business because it is convertible into cash once the invoice is sent and the receivable is paid. And since all receivables are payable within 12 months, they are all considered current assets. Here's how it works: When an order is shipped, it gets captured as net revenue on the Net Income Statement and as a receivable under the current asset category on the Balance Sheet. When that invoice is finally paid, receivables goes down and cash goes up on the Balance Sheet. Total assets on the left side of the Balance Sheet will remain the same, they just shifted categories. The Balance Sheet will reflect this.

The Cash Flow Statement will also show that inflow of cash, but remember, the Cash Flow Statement only reflects cash transactions, so it is blind to the money owed the business but not paid yet. (Stay tuned, because in Chapter 9 you see how all three work together to help you make good business decisions.)

Only the Balance Sheet captures accounts receivable. It's good that something is keeping track of these, because they need to be closely managed to ensure that the business gets paid fully and on time. Remember Susie, the payables clerk from the previous chapter? Your receivable is her payable.

Weeks can pass between the time a client buys something and the time it pays its bills. A lot can go wrong between these two events. That's why knowing what receivables are, which ones are aging, and managing them closely is one of the keys to maintaining a healthy cash position for the business. It's also why we spent a dog's age talking about specific ways to manage invoices in the previous chapter.

A "note receivable," money the company loaned out that needs to be paid back within that 12-month window, might also be included among current assets, though notes are relatively rare.

Inventory Inventory is a current asset because it's convertible into cash within 12 months, at least in theory. It's always valued at the cost of direct materials and direct labor required to produce a finished product. In short, inventory is always valued at cost of goods sold (COGS).

Managing inventory can be pretty tricky business. The first thing you have to know is that *inventory is nothing more than big piles of cash sitting on a shelf in a warehouse.* If you didn't have the inventory, what would you have? You'd have the cash.

Managing inventory is a balancing act. If the business carries too little inventory, it can't satisfy all the demand for its products because it can't ship the orders and invoice the customer to get paid. As a result, net revenue, gross margin, and cash levels all suffer. When inventory is too low, cash potential is not reached because there's not enough available product to sell. This is a *supply problem.*

When inventory is too high, this can also create major cash problems, especially if the business sells seasonal or perishable inventory that has a finite shelf life. If inventory is much higher than demand for the product, too much cash went into manufacturing it and the sales are not there to convert it into net revenue and then back into cash. This is considered a *demand problem.*

That's why it's important to keep inventory levels as low as possible while satisfying customer demand. If the business has to throw out spoiled or marked-down out-of-season inventory, it still has paid for the cost of manufacturing it.

At the end of the day, either unbalanced situation is a result of inaccurate forecasting. Although no one can predict exactly what demand will be, here are some considerations that will help you manage inventory levels.

Effective inventory management has to do with matching as closely as possible the timing and quantity of the inventory to actual demand. You want to squeeze the lag time between the time a product is produced and a sale is made. The only way to achieve that without a crystal ball is to do everything possible to reduce the amount of time it takes to build inventory.

As customers indicate their true interest in a product, it's always easier and less risky to build inventory based on what demand actually is, or **real demand**, instead of what you hope it's going to be, or **forecasted demand**. "Responsiveness"—squeezing time out of the inventory process—is the only way to do this. Those companies that can produce inventory on demand are usually very profitable.

Once customers provide real feedback on what they want and how much of it they want to buy, then it's time to trigger the inventory-making machinery. The less time it takes to build inventory, the less of it you need on hand at any point in time. The less inventory on hand, the more efficient the use of cash. Smaller batches built with greater frequency will always produce better cash flow and fewer excess or inadequate inventory problems. And that better cash flow will outweigh any benefit of the cost savings you might have gotten from *economies of scale* (purchasing raw material in large quantities cheaper, paying your suppliers less per item for a larger run, and the like).

If you had to err on higher versus lower inventory levels, I would err on the side of lower inventory levels, especially in a soft economy. Cash needs to be viewed and managed as the finite, precious resource it is. Cash is not king, it's emperor. Don't take it for granted. If a product you carry is sold out in a flash, that's a good thing. While losing some sales due to inadequate inventory levels is painful, it's still better than having paid for inventory that doesn't sell.

What you want to avoid at all costs is *returns*! Returns are, as Don Corleone would say, *il bacio della morte*—the kiss of death.

No business wins when merchandise has to be returned. It costs money to pack and ship it back. It costs money to warehouse it. It costs money to insure it and to take physical inventory at the end of the year (which the IRS requires). Inventory can also get damaged during any of these stages. And, like the rest of us, inventory rarely increases in perceived value as it ages. In short, it's a bear.

Another thing about building large volumes of inventory is that it's always very difficult to know which products are going to sell well. We think we know, but honestly, the customer is always filled with surprises.

My company, Bedazzled Inc., sold screen-printed T-shirts. There was a butterfly T-shirt, and a picnic T-shirt. I thought the picnic T-shirt would sell best. I was wrong. The butterfly T-shirt was much more popular. Who knew? Well, in fact, I could have (should have!) taken a survey of my best friends. Or even asked random strangers at the entrance to the subway. Almost anything would have been smarter than just assuming I knew.

One of the most brilliant schemes to strike the balance between having adequate inventory to sell but not too much that the cash position was compromised was developed by the Bonobos Company, which sells made-to-order men's casual pants. The entire customer experience is quite different from the average department store.

First the company creates one sample of each product in the line in all the sizes available. Customers make appointments, they try on the samples in a lovely showroom so they get personal attention, the customer places an order (and pays for it on the spot with a credit card), and Bonobos builds inventory and ships directly to the customer's door. The customer usually waits several weeks to get their order because the company aggregates customer orders before it instructs the factory to build inventory.

The beauty of this system is that cash is not squandered on inventory that won't sell. The biggest investment in inventory Bonobos makes is the manufacturing of the samples. That's expensive on a per piece basis, but doesn't compare to how expensive it would be if the company attempted to guess what demand would be by size and model and went ahead and built inventory, only to get it wrong and have to digest leftovers no one wanted. As demand for these great-looking pants grows, it's likely inventory management practices will change and they'll start taking some larger risks in building inventory in anticipation of demand. In the early years when cash is tight, this build-on-demand inventory management process makes perfect sense. It's great risk management.

What are the most important things to remember about inventory management?

- Test the market with samples first, if you can, to know what is really going to sell.

- If possible, don't build inventory in large quantities and eat up cash unless the business has the orders in its hands.

- Try to find strategic partners that have quick turn-arounds for building inventory.

- Unless you have real-time data on customer demand and have an extremely tight connection to your suppliers, you'll never get inventory forecasting exactly right.

- Err on the side of less rather than more inventory as a rule of thumb.

- If you have to make a trade-off between paying more per unit in COGS to reduce the cycle time to build inventory, choose the higher COGS and reduced production time. You'll be placing smaller orders with greater frequency, turning inventory faster and cash faster. Read this point again—it's not very complicated (place smaller orders, more frequently), but it's really, *really* important for managing your inventory.

Here's an illustration of this last point. If the time to build inventory is cut from six weeks to one week, in theory, the business will only need one-sixth the inventory it would normally need because the production line can move more quickly. That means the business locks up a lot less total cash in that inventory purchase. As inventory is sold, the supplier can replenish it faster if its production line is set up to do this. This makes the use of cash a lot more efficient. It also means the supplier can produce more of the most popular items so the risk of leftover inventory and returns is lower. Will the unit cost be higher? Yes. It's okay to pay more per unit as long as the new COGS is low enough to ensure at least a 30 percent gross margin on those items. You're essentially paying for the time you're saving. I believe it's worth it and will arm-wrestle any CPA who says otherwise.

Why am I spending so much time discussing inventory management? Because too many small business managers get it terribly wrong. If inventory levels are too high and the business runs out of cash, it could be the end of the road.

Service businesses do not have the inventory management challenge that product businesses do. The "inventory" that service businesses need to manage is time. The constraint here is the 24-hour day, which we spoke about in Chapter 3.

Fixed Assets Assets that are not easily converted into cash within 12 months—buildings, land, equipment, computers, and furniture, for example—are placed under the **fixed asset** category. This category is affectionately called, "property, plant, and equipment" or "PPE" for short. Plant and equipment will eventually have to be replaced, so they depreciate in value each year and that depreciation shows up as an annual expense on the Net Income Statement, but the cumulative expense, from the date these assets were purchased, shows up on the Balance Sheet. (The Net Income Statement only shows the expense for one calendar year, while the Balance Sheet shows the cumulative effects of what has taken place since the original purchase of that plant and equipment.)

Here are a few things to remember about the nature of a fixed asset. Just because an asset—for example, a building—may *fluctuate* in value, it doesn't mean that asset doesn't have value. Asset values as recorded on a balance sheet may fluctuate based on many factors, including changes in technology, shifts in the local supply and demand for real estate, and shifts in interest rates and rates of depreciation. Your accountant will know how to properly capture asset values and depreciation expenses. (Each small business is different, so I won't attempt to go over all the "what if" scenarios in here.)

What's important to know is that the difference between a current and a fixed asset is that 12-month time frame it takes to convert an asset into cash by selling it. Fixed assets take longer to sell and convert to cash.

Fixed assets also tend to be large purchases that have cash value but are not easily convertible into cash (that 12-month period is the sticking point). Most fixed assets, with the exception of property (land, that is, not the buildings on it), are depreciable assets. The value of a fixed asset on the Balance Sheet will reflect its purchase price less the total depreciation that has been taken (by your accountant) on that asset from the time it was purchased. (We looked at depreciation in some detail in both Chapters 2 and 5.) In other words, you'll see a net asset value on the Balance Sheet for a building or a piece of equipment that will equal the purchase price minus the accumulated depreciation.

That covers the asset side of the Balance Sheet equation. That's everything the business owns.

Since every ying has a yang, let's now review the liabilities side of the Balance Sheet.

Liabilities

Liabilities will be found on the right-hand side of the Balance Sheet, which shows everything the business owes. These are the obligations of the business and, just as assets are split into current assets and fixed assets, liabilities are split into current liabilities and long-term liabilities. Figure 7–4 shows most liability categories you might come across on a Balance Sheet.

Current Liabilities A business' obligations that need to be paid within 12 months are called **current liabilities**. These include accounts payable, notes payable, and credit lines payable. We'll look at them one at a time.

Accounts Payable Invoices from suppliers for goods that have been shipped or services that have been rendered are called **accounts payable** (or "payables"). If the business keeps its accounts payable current—that is, if bills get paid on a timely basis—it will earn real points with suppliers when they must be asked for a favor. As you saw when I discussed managing cash in Chapter 5, it's important to keep track of accounts payable because the obligation to the business is very real.

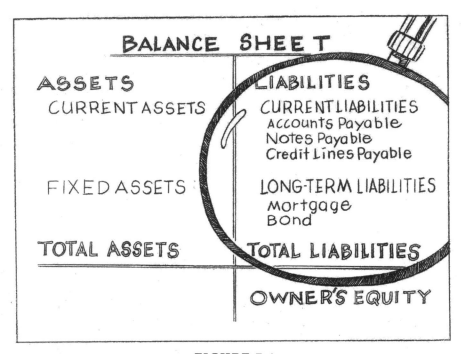

FIGURE 7-4

Managing cash matters because accounts payable is satisfied or paid with it. As you cut checks to pay outstanding bills, accounts payables on the liabilities side of the Balance Sheet goes down—as does the current asset cash—by exactly the same amount. The Balance Sheet will reflect this. The Cash Flow Statement will also indicate cash has gone out of the business, but only the Balance Sheet shows the whole story. The good news is that, even though cash, a current asset, has gone down, so has a current liability, namely, accounts payable. The owner's equity, or net worth of the business, is unchanged. You'll soon see why.

A very successful entrepreneur tells a story about the early days of launching his business. He and his partners would drive over the state line and mail the checks to their suppliers from the neighboring state because they knew it took an extra day or two to reach the supplier. That gave the company an extra day or two of operating cash before these checks cleared. That's how tight the cash position was at the beginning. Most businesses will have difficulty paying all their bills at one time or another. It's part of the business cycle.

Notes Payable Short-term obligations to investors, suppliers, or the bank to cover cash crunches or to build inventory are called **notes payable**. These are short-term, not long-term, obligations. They typically must be paid within 12 months.

Credit Lines Payable If you've ever owned a credit card, you have a good idea of how a credit line works. Credit lines are essentially the same thing without the plastic. **Credit lines payable** is where you'll find another set of short-term obligations. Banks and suppliers will extend credit to credit-worthy customers. Typically, these are revolving lines of credit. The business can use some or all of the credit line. As it gets paid back, the credit line opens up again. If you own a checking account and have a strong credit rating, you can apply for **overdraft protection**. This is a short-term loan the bank makes to your account if there are insufficient funds to cover those checks. The bank will honor the checks, allowing you to avoid all the bounced check fees and embarrassment, but it will also charge you interest on the loan for that month. The bank also expects overdrafts to be repaid each month. Overdrafts are a liability or an obligation of the business until it's paid. If it isn't paid like clockwork, watch how fast the bank's mission control shuts down the overdraft protection.

Credit cards are also a form of revolving credit. Those that are used on behalf of the business for travel and incidentals will receive monthly statements indicating what's owed on the account. My advice is that these should be paid in *full* every month when the bill comes due. The interest rates on credit cards can be so astronomical that while they're convenient, they can sink the ship if not managed properly.

Hard to believe? Try this.

I conduct seminars called "Accounting for the Numberphobic." They are aimed at small business owner/managers, and registering for the seminar also includes a one-on-one meeting with each participant to review their Net Income Statements and their Cash Flow Statements.

When I looked at one participant's Net Income Statement, I almost stopped breathing. On it was a line item that jumped off the page. It was the interest expense of $50,000 he paid in a single year. The business was only generating $200,000, so the only way interest expense could be so stratospherically high for this little company was if he was financing the business on his credit cards. Only credit card companies can charge double-digit interest rates. That racks up pretty darn fast.

Guess how much was outstanding on five different credit cards? Would you believe $400,000? No, I'm not kidding. It took years to dig such a deep and scary financial hole.

The problem beneath the problem for this small business manager was twofold. The first problem was that his gross margins were only 15 percent, not the 30 percent we recommend. They were too low, so the more he sold, the more credit he needed to fill the gap between what the business was generating in cash flow and what was required to build inventory and to pay the bills. In short, the more he sold, the deeper the financial hole in which he found himself.

The second problem was that as soon as he had trouble paying off his credit card debt every month, he should have realized something was wrong and gotten help. If all you can afford to pay is the minimum payment each month, you will never dig your way out of that ditch. Never. Never ever! Minimum payments on credit cards never cover the full rate of interest that is due, never mind paying down some of the original loan, or principal. If the business can't afford to pay off the credit card every month, it can't afford the purchase. That's tough love. It'll also keep the business from stumbling beyond the point of return.

I have no idea who this guy's accountant was, but it was horrifying to think any CPA could sign off on this kind of self-destructive credit line management behavior for over nine years and say nothing to prevent the situation from getting as bad as it did. And yes, the business eventually had to declare bankruptcy.

Credit lines are not for the faint of heart. They should be used sparingly and only for short-term use when you know the cash is coming in. If the business needs to buy time because there's a significant lag between when cash needs to go out and when it's expected to arrive, then credit lines from the bank should be considered, not credit cards.

The interest rates on a bank credit line will be far more favorable than the interest rates on credit cards. Are credit cards more convenient? Yes. Does it take more effort to apply for a credit line at the bank? Absolutely. That extra effort up front will save the business tons of cash, however, and if done right, can get the business on a solid footing without forfeiting financial soundness. In Chapter 8, I give you an insider's view on how to manage the banking relationship so getting a credit line does not feel like torture—and you will learn how to avoid the mistakes other small business managers have made when they apply for a credit line.

One last word on current liabilities: If the business employs full-time or part-time staff, there may be an additional line on the Balance Sheet called **salaries payable**. It's money that's been earned by the employees but not paid yet by the business. Just know what it is and if it pops up sometime, you'll understand it.

Long-Term Liabilities

Mortgages and bonds fall into the category of long-term liabilities.

A **mortgage** is typically a long-term liability that is paid back, with mountains of interest, over several decades. As the monthly mortgage is paid, which will include interest on the loan as well as principal owed, the "mortgage outstanding" will decrease on the Balance Sheet. (Principal is simply the value of the original loan less any principal that has been repaid.) In other words, as the liability is satisfied month after month, in small increments, the outstanding liability gets smaller. The equity or ownership in the building goes up. If the business owes less to the bank on the building, it means it owns more equity in the building. You may understand this in terms of a home mortgage (my apartment in Manhattan). In terms of the Balance Sheet, it may look more complicated, but it's just as straightforward. Your cash goes down from paying the mortgage, your long-term liabilities line goes down because now the business owes less on the mortgage, and, on the other side of the Balance Sheet, the value of your fixed assets goes up because equity in the building has gone up. This is what you want.

If the building is sold for more than the value of the remaining mortgage, then the outstanding mortgage loan can be satisfied with the proceeds from the purchasers. If you're lucky, there will be some money left over.

A **bond** is a debt instrument that formalizes a loan between a lender and a borrower. Each bond will reflect the amount owed and payment terms for that specific loan. A bond is an asset (receivable) to the lender and a liability (payable) to the borrower. Bonds tend to be long-term debt instruments that are usually backed by collateral in case the borrower does not pay back the loan. You will rarely see a line item for "Bonds Payable" on a small business Balance Sheet. Just know what it is in case you do.

Owner's Equity

You might hear owner's equity referred to as **shareholder's equity**. They mean the same thing; this number is always found on the right-hand side of the Balance Sheet. Even though owner's equity shows up right under liabilities, it is not a liability; it is simply what's left over after liabilities have been deducted from assets (what's left after you've subtracted what the business owes from what the business owns). This section includes equity investments and retained earnings (which is cumulative net income less any distributions).

Equity Investments

If a business owner invests capital into a business, which in almost all cases happens when it is being launched, then that capital will show up, under owner's equity, as an **equity investment**. Here's where you see the $30,000 in start-up money that you saved (and borrowed from your parents), and the $5,000 from your husband. These infusions of cash will also increase the current assets on the Balance Sheet. Cash goes up and owner's equity goes up, initially, so the scale stays balanced. Figure 7–5 shows the owner's equity section of a Balance Sheet.

Retained Earnings

If you add up all the net income that has been generated by the business since inception, then deduct any dividends or owner's or investor's draw (see below) paid out, you'll get **retained earnings**. Retained earnings are cumulative and the only place you'll see them is on the right side of the Balance Sheet under the owner's equity section. Retained earnings will only show up if cumulative net income is positive. Now you know how to determine that by looking at Net Income Statements over time.

Don't stress too much about retained earnings. Just know what it is and where it shows up on the Balance Sheet.

Owner's and Investor's Draw

There is one more line that may appear under the owner's equity section. Owners of businesses structured as sole proprietors and partnerships can legally pay themselves by taking money out of the

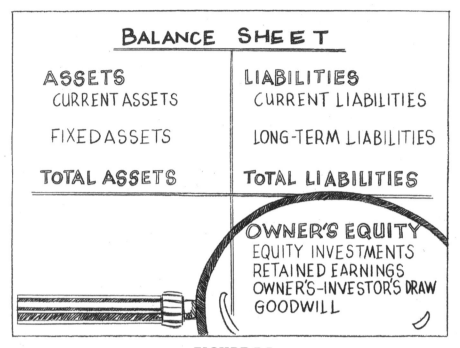

FIGURE 7-5

business not as salary but as **owner's draw** or **investor's draw**. Owners report this as income and pay taxes on it so they are free to take out as much or as little as they choose. If the business does not have predictable net revenue, owners may choose to take an owner's draw from the balance sheet instead of committing the business to paying a steady monthly salary, which would show up in the "Sales, General, and Administrative" section of the net income statement.

Good Will
Every now and then you'll see something called "Good Will" in the owner's equity section of the Balance Sheet. **Good will** has to do with the monetary value of a brand name. If a company, like Apple

Computer, has managed to create a world-class name that is so compelling people will buy its products on that basis alone, then you have brand equity. Vernon Hill, the genius who launched Commerce Bank in the United States and Metro Bank in the United Kingdom, says that when the company and the customer become one, you have an emotional brand. Emotional brands have rabid fans. Emotional brands have monetary value.

As a manager of a small business, you probably don't have brand equity. Don't worry; just know what it is so if you do see it, listed usually on the Balance Sheet of a publicly traded company, you'll know what it means.

* * *

The Balance Sheet is wonderful for revealing a lot of the hidden things the Net Income Statement and the Cash Flow Statement don't show, like receivables, current and fixed assets, payables, long-term liabilities, and owner's equity. It is also useful for capturing the cumulative performance of the business since the beginning. In contrast, the Net Income Statement and Cash Flow Statement usually reveal monthly or annual totals.

Total assets and total liabilities are really easy to see on the Balance Sheet. It's easy to note relationships between current assets and current liabilities and know if the business can cover immediate cash needs in the next 12 months. The Cash Flow Statement helps to do this, but the Balance Sheet provides the fuller picture.

Isn't it also comforting to know that the business you manage can be worth a lot more than just the salvage value of the desks and computers? It's possible to build real equity into the value of a business that you can eventually sell, hopefully for a premium, to another adventure seeker who wants to see the business thrive. Remember, the entire business itself can be an asset if the Balance Sheet is strong and owner's equity is growing. Any lender or investor will be attracted to such a Balance Sheet. It's the *Reader's Digest* version of the business. In Chapter 8, we'll peer into a bank's back office and see how they think and how they will look at your Balance Sheet. Most small business managers have no idea how to optimize their banking relationships. After reading this book, you won't be one of those.

KEY TAKEAWAYS

▶ The Balance Sheet captures cumulative effects of operations in a snapshot. It's an efficient way to see the cumulative effects of how the company is building net worth through operations over time.

▶ Use either of the following formulas to determine the net worth of a business:

$$\text{Assets} = \text{Liabilities} + \text{Owner's Equity}$$
$$\text{Assets} - \text{Liabilities} = \text{Owner's Equity}$$

▶ The left side of the Balance Sheet shows current assets—cash, accounts receivable, and inventory—and fixed assets—land, buildings, equipment, furniture, and computers.

▶ Total assets are derived by adding up the values of current assets and fixed assets.

▶ The right side of the Balance Sheet shows current liabilities—accounts payable, notes payable, credit lines payable, and salaries payable—and long-term liabilities—mortgages or other debts with a term longer than 12 months.

▶ Total liabilities are derived by adding up the values of current liabilities and long-term liabilities.

▶ Owner's equity (net worth) consists of the owner's investment in the company and the retained earnings (cumulative net income that has been reinvested in the business) minus any owner's or investor's draw.

CHAPTER **8**

The Balance
Sheet in Action
How to Win Friends and Influence Bankers

What I've been showing you throughout this book is how to build a business that is a going concern, an accounting term that CPAs and bankers use to describe a well-run, profitable business that isn't under threat of bankruptcy in the foreseeable future. A **going concern** is a business that is self-sustaining with predictable revenue streams, reasonable expenses, and adequate cash levels to pay its bills. Building such a business must be the goal of every small business owner/manager.

In order to help you build a going concern, I needed to take you through the building blocks of your financial dashboard—the Net Income Statement, the Cash Flow Statement, and the Balance

Sheet—first, so that you could tell if the business you manage is, or has the potential to be, a going concern.

The Balance Sheet provides searing insight here. In this chapter I describe what happens to assets, liabilities, and owner's equity when you apply the advice from previous chapters to the business you manage, and I'll introduce you to just a few key ratios bankers look at that indicate whether the business's debt levels are manageable or are entering a danger zone and need to be addressed fast.

The cool thing about the Balance Sheet is it captures the results of *all* the activities of running the business from the day the business opened its doors. That's why bankers love it so much and why they home in on it first, when a business applies for a credit line or a long-term loan. And that's what this chapter is about: how you can get a business loan from a bank.

Now you're going to learn how to think like a banker. This will dramatically improve your chances of being approved for a credit line or a long-term loan.

Every small business needs a solid banking relationship, so it's important to make your banker a strategic partner in the success of the business—maybe not your new BFF, but certainly an ally. Believe it or not, your banker is on your side!

I interviewed some very senior bankers to get their perspective, and this chapter will give you the inside scoop.

WHAT THE BALANCE SHEET NUMBERS REVEAL

You were introduced to the Balance Sheet in Chapter 7, and here it is again. This time we're going to dig a little deeper into what the numbers on the Balance Sheet mean. To do so, let's see what's going on at XYZ Company (see Figure 8–1). As you learned, there are only three major categories: assets (current and fixed), liabilities (current and long term), and owner's equity. We've added numerical values for each so you clearly see the relationship between them.

XYZ Company
Balance Sheet

Assets		Liabilities	
Current Assets		Current Liabilities	
Cash	$110,000	Accounts Payable	$9,000
Inventory	$5,000	Line of Credit	$1,000
Accounts Receivables	$5,000		
Fixed Assets		**Long-Term Liabilities**	
PPE	$100,000	Mortgages	$50,000
Less: Cumulative Depreciation	($20,000)		
Total Assets	**$200,000**	**Total Liabilities**	**$60,000**
		Owner's Equity	
		Retained Earnings	$60,000
		Equity Investments	$80,000
		Total Liabilities and Equity	**$200,000**

FIGURE 8–1

First, take a look at current assets, specifically, the cash position of the business. It's half the value of total assets. XYZ has a very large cash position ($110,000). That cash is available right now to pay bills or to grow the business. It's the most liquid asset the business has. But just looking at the cash position doesn't tell us everything we need to know about the health of XYZ. We want to know whether all current assets taken together can cover current liabilities, if necessary. Adding up $110,000 in cash and $10,000 in inventory and accounts receivable, total current assets are $120,000. These are cash or convertible to cash within 12 months.

Now look at current liabilities. These are obligations the business has to pay back within 12 months. There are two categories here: accounts payable and line of credit. They total $10,000 in current liabilities. Every bank will want to know if XYZ Company has adequate **working capital**, current assets minus current liabilities, to cover current liabilities.

We figured out current assets are $120,000 and current liabilities are $10,000, so the business has $110,000 of working capital to keep the place humming. This is a nice strong position for the business. XYZ Company can pay off the mortgage and the current liabilities with just the cash that's in the bank and still have $50,000 left over. Inventory looks a little low, though, so it's possible that some of that cash will be used to build more inventory in the near future. The good news is, XYZ probably will not have to take on any debt to buy that inventory with such a healthy cash position.

The risk that this company will not be able to pay its expenses and satisfy its liabilities appears to be very low. We know the managers of this business have not taken on more debt than the business can safely and easily pay back.

If we wanted to see what owner's equity, or net worth, is for this business, we can get there two ways: The first way is to add up retained earnings and equity investments, which total $140,000.

Owner's Equity = Retained Earnings + Equity Investments

Owner's Equity = $60,000 + $80,000 = $140,000

The second way we can derive this number is equally straightforward; we can simply deduct total liabilities from total assets. No surprise, we get to the same number: $140,000.

$$\text{Total Assets} - \text{Total Liabilities} = \text{Owner's Equity}$$
$$\$200,000 - \$60,000 = \$140,000$$

Be aware that if you open an accounting book, you may find this same equation in yet a different version, which we show below (you may remember it from the previous chapter). As you can see, in order to isolate owner's equity, we have subtracted the value of the total liabilities from both sides of the equation to find the value of owner's equity:

$$\text{Total Assets} = \text{Total Liabilities} + \text{Owner's Equity}$$
$$\$200,000 = \$60,000 + \text{Owner's Equity}$$
$$\$200,000 - \$60,000 = \$140,000$$

In Chapter 7, when you were introduced to the equation Assets = Liabilities + Owner's Equity (and its variations), the word "Total" was implied. Mathematically, all these equations are the same.

HOW TO IMPROVE YOUR BALANCE SHEET

Unfortunately, most small business owners do not have a Balance Sheet anywhere near as healthy as the XYZ Company's. So, now that you understand more fully the significance of the Balance Sheet, let me offer some suggestions as to how you can improve your own.

To strengthen the Balance Sheet you either have to increase assets faster than liabilities or simply decrease liabilities with the same asset base. Here are three of the most important ideas you learned about in earlier chapters that will help improve your Balance Sheet.

Raise Your Gross Margin to 30 Percent or Greater

If you can raise your current gross margin to 30 percent or higher, the business will reach the breakeven point faster and require less cash from loans to grow the business profitably. The premium the business captures between the selling price and COGS is greater, so when a client pays an outstanding invoice, the receivable converts into a cash payment with a higher gross margin. That new, higher gross margin becomes more cash for the business—and the Balance Sheet will look better.

It's also easier to finance the purchase of new inventory from the cash generated by the business instead of having to take out a loan to finance it. So as gross margin rises, cash increases on every sale. If the invoicing and collections process at the business is organized, then that higher gross margin locked up in accounts receivable converts into more cash more often and at a faster rate.

Invoice on a Timely Basis and Manage the Collections Process

If you do this as a weekly business discipline, the amount of cash you have in the business on the asset side of the Balance Sheet will be higher. It means the business generates more cash by itself, and needs less from loans or outside investors.

Cash in the bank will increase, accounts receivable will decrease, and—at least in theory—you will need less cash from credit lines to run the business. And as the line of credit (under liabilities) decreases, owner's equity will increase. Accounts receivable decreases as customers pay the business, but cash increases by the same amount, so current assets might be the same, but as liabilities go down, owner's equity goes up. This is what you want.

Keep All Expenses as Low as Possible for as Long as Possible

Keeping expenses low also helps the business reach the breakeven point faster and become self-sustaining sooner. Net revenue (with your new 30 percent or better gross margin) can cover all fixed and variable expenses—and again, there should be little need for outside sources of funding to run the business if customers pay their bills. Keeping expenses low should keep current liabilities in check and increase owner's equity, assuming assets stay the same. If assets go up while liabilities go down, the business will be approaching Nirvana.

HOW A BANK EVALUATES A BUSINESS

When you take your car to be inspected, the car mechanic always goes through the same routine of making sure certain key indicators are functioning properly. The bank does the same thing when reviewing businesses before it approves a loan. A superstar in the banking world, who asked to go unnamed, explained the review process all her loan officers go through before the bank extends credit to a small business.

Here's the step-by-step procedure:

- *The bank tests to see if the business is a going concern.* The key test of whether or not a business is a going concern is if it has a stable and loyal client base, predictable profitability, and predictable cash flow. First, the bank will look at the Net Income Statement of the business for at least a full year, maybe two, broken out month by month. It wants to see if the business is making a profit. You know how to do that too after reading the first three chapters of this book.

- *Then the bank looks at net margin percentage.* This is simply net income divided by net revenue multiplied by 100. You'll find net income (bottom line) and net revenue (top line), also on the Net Income Statement. When you divide net income by net revenue you discover how much of each dollar of net revenue drops to the bottom line as profit. Remember, we said for the average corner grocery store, the percentage of net margin is typically only about 2 percent? Well, each industry has standards for net margin percentage and you should know what the standard is in your industry. That makes you an informed business banking client. If the net margin percentage for the small business you manage is higher than the industry average, you win points with any banker. (Here's a URL you can use for a quick peek: http://pages.stern.nyu.edu/~%20adamodar/New_Home_Page/datafile/margin.html. No guarantees that your industry will be listed exactly as you conceive it, but it's a pretty substantial list.)

- *Next, the bank will look at gross margin to see if it is adequate to pay fixed and variable expenses.* All expenses, including interest on both short- and long-term debt, are paid out of gross margin, as you may recall. This too is found on the Net Income Statement under variable expenses. If gross margin is 30 percent or higher, the bank will likely conclude you've done a great job at pricing and keeping the direct variable costs (the COGS) under control. Chapter 3 did a deep dive on what to do to raise gross margin if the business you manage isn't there yet.

- *The bank will also want to know if revenue will continue to grow or dry up.* Reviewing the quality of your client base will be important in answering this question. In Chapter 5 we compared the client bases of Jane's and Joe's Hardware. One business has a diversified client base, the other did not. The bank will look at client purchasing behavior as well. Have your bookkeeper prepare a report that shows what percentage of clients have been with the business at least two years and how many are new clients who just purchased this calendar year. Do clients purchase on a regular basis and do they stay with your business for the long haul? Your banker knows customer loyalty drives repeat purchases and referrals to new customers. That drives net revenue. A series of Net Income Statements showing growth of net revenue gives the bank confidence in your future.

• *The bank will look at how well the business converts outstanding invoices into cash.* The Cash Flow Statement will provide good insights here. The bank will look at the cash flow cycle of the business, which we discussed in Chapter 5. The cash cycle charts the time lag between when the business has to pay its bills and when clients pay the business. My banking honcho referred to that as "financing the accounts receivable/accounts payable time gap." The bank wants to see how effective you are in collecting money owed the business. That's why we spent so much time talking about easy techniques for doing this in Chapter 6.

• *The bank will look at the size of working capital.* It will look at the Balance Sheet to compare assets to liabilities to determine if the business is able to pay the interest and principle on additional current or long-term debt, as we just did for XYZ Company. It will deduct inventory from current assets and see if the most liquid assets, namely cash and accounts receivables, are adequate to cover current liabilities. It's a type of "what if" scenario testing to help the bank determine whether, in a worst-case scenario, the business will be able to meet its obligations even if inventory cannot be converted into net revenue and, ultimately, cash.

- *Last but not least, the bank will look carefully at the key players in the business.* It will want to know the history and background of the managers who run the day-to-day operations. Subject-matter expertise, years of experience, and longevity with the business all count favorably when asking for any kind of bank loan. Banks know that teams that have worked successfully together for years are more successful at running profitable businesses over time.

DURATION OF A LOAN AND THE ROLE OF COLLATERAL

Bankers are pragmatists. They want to know how the loan will be paid back, when it will be paid back, and what collateral is available—in the unhappy event the business fails—that can be liquidated (sold) to pay off the loan. Make your loan request easier for the banker to agree to.

Match the Expected Life of the Asset with the Length of the Loan

If you need to finance a current asset—the creation of inventory, for instance—you can finance it with a current liability, that is, a short-term loan, such as a credit line from a bank. Another short-term loan option is to apply for credit from the supplier making the inventory—but you would usually need to have an established, long-running relationship for this. In either event, this credit line would show up in the accounts payable line on the Balance Sheet.

The logic that holds true for financing short-term assets also holds true for long-term assets. If you're buying a building that might have a 30-year useful life, you'd finance that with a long-term mortgage. This will show up on the Balance Sheet as a long-term liability.

Collateral Greases the Skids

If you already have a signed order from a customer who wants to buy this inventory, getting a loan from the bank or the supplier will be much easier. When I ran Bedazzled, Inc., I approached the bank for a Small Business Administration loan with the purchase order from a reputable local retailer in my hand. That reduced the risk for the bank dramatically. The order becomes **collateral** against the short-term debt.

Collateral is something that is convertible into cash, in this case, a receivable, that is pledged against a loan. It can be liquidated should the business default on paying the loan back. If the business taking out the loan can't pay it back, the lender can sell the receivable to recover some or all of the remaining principal from the loan. Maintaining a strong Balance Sheet where assets are larger than liabilities will always make it easier to negotiate with the bank.

EIGHT MYTHS ABOUT DEALING WITH BANKS

The one thing my banking expert said that surprised me was how naive managers of even multimillion-dollar small businesses are when dealing with banks. Let's make sure you are among the savvy set. Here are eight myths small business managers believe, followed by the truth from the banking expert's point of view.

> ***Myth #1:*** *The bank just needs to know my business needs working capital. As long as my Balance Sheet is strong, the bank doesn't care how the business uses the money from the loan.*
>
> **Truth #1:** Not true. The bank will ask you specifically how you intend to use the cash from the loan and whether or not it is short term. You need to have a thoughtful answer. If you don't, the bank will fill the gap with negative assumptions. Bankers are institutionalized pessimists. Do you need the cash to build inventory? That's called "supply chain financing." Do you need to finance payroll while the business collects payments from customers who owe it money? That's called "payroll financing." Does the business need to invest in infrastructure to grow? That's called "capitalization financing." Why does the loan purpose matter? Because what the business is financing will determine the terms of the loan. Have a clear understanding of why the business needs the money and how that loan will strengthen the Balance Sheet for the business, that is, how the loan will help grow the assets of the business.

Myth #2: *All bank loans are the same.*

Truth #2: You knew this one wasn't true. My source talked about "revolvers"—revolving lines of credit that need to be paid back every 30 days. They're like a charge card but with a lower interest rate. Once the loan is paid back, the credit line is available again to the business— but only after another 30 days have passed before tapping the credit line again. Other loans, like those for purchasing or renovating office space, can be longer term with completely different payback schedules and interest rates. These loans act more like mortgage loans, though they tend to be shorter in duration with higher interest costs because there's more risk associated with them.

Myth #3: *Once the loan is approved, the bank doesn't care what happens as long as the business pays the loan back.*

Truth #3: Once a bank issues a loan, it becomes the silent partner to the business. Partners always want to know how the business is performing. You know all those requirements the business needed to meet to get the loan in the first place? The bank wants to make sure those financials for the business remain strong over time. The obligation of the business doesn't end with paying the interest expense and the principal on the loan. That's expected. The bank will require quarterly and annual reviews of the business's financials too. Be prepared for this.

Myth #4: *The business functions as a separate entity from the owner's personal life, so the bank doesn't care about the business owner's personal Balance Sheet.*

Truth #4: Not true. The bank takes a holistic view of the owners and managers of small businesses. That means even though the business may run as a separate legal entity, the bank might require personal guarantees of privately owned collateral (your house, your first-born, your wife's jewelry, your vehicle) to release the loan to the business. If a business owner is a doctor, dentist, or lawyer, this is quite common.

Myth #5: If the business is showing a loss, the bank will still extend a loan if cash flow is positive.

Truth: #5: Nice try, but no. If the small business manager is trying to reduce taxes by showing a loss on the Net Income Statement, that's a problem when applying for a loan from a bank. It's important to show cash flow *and* profits. If you want a loan for $1.00, the bank wants you to show at least $1.35 in net income to prove you can cover the loan in a weak economic environment to reduce loan default risk. The challenge here is the tug of war with the IRS. Some small business owners try to front-load expenses to reduce profits so they can pay less in taxes (and this can be perfectly legal). Just remember that tax reduction strategies in the short term may work against the business if you want to apply for a loan with a bank or if you eventually want to sell a business.

Myth #6: The bank does not look at retained earnings on the Balance Sheet.

Truth #6: Retained earnings is a number scrutinized by a lender. Retained earnings is found in the owner's equity portion on the Balance Sheet. It connects the Net Income Statement to the Balance Sheet because this number reflects the cumulative net income the business has generated since its inception. The small business manager can choose to retain the net income—the profit—in the business or to distribute it. There is a problem with distributing all of the earnings, however, instead of keeping some of it in the business (as retained earnings) for future expansion. Again, the $1.00 loan/$1.35 ratio holds here. Let that ratio be your guide on how much of the business profits should be distributed at the end of the year. If you are planning to apply for a loan later on, keep as much cash and retained earnings in the business as you can before you apply. And know that it is a common requirement from commercial lenders that you keep the cash and the retained earnings on the Balance Sheet for at least 90 days after the loan proceeds are received. Distributing profits to owners is perfectly legal, but if you take all the cash out of the business, the bank will not grant your loan.

Myth #7: The bank only cares about my business relationship.

Truth #7: The bank cares about *all* your banking needs. If you have sizable personal accounts elsewhere, offering to bring them to the lending bank can give you not-insignificant negotiating leverage when applying for a business loan.

Myth #8: If the business I manage does a lot of transactions with the bank, I'm considered a large customer.

Truth #8: Your banking relationship is primarily measured by the size of the balances the business keeps in the bank—not the number of transactions that flow through the account. The bank makes money on deposits, not just transactions. The higher the balances the business keeps at the bank, the more leverage it has with the bank.

Now that we've dispelled some myths, let me offer you two lists: one of do's and one of don'ts. They may seem like a lot to understand, but they're important. Following them has the potential to save you a great deal of time and money.

Do's When Working with a Bank

- Know what a "going concern" is and how to prove the small business you manage is one of them.

- Develop a deep understanding of your client base. Is it diversified? Stable? Predictable?

- Hire a crackerjack bookkeeper to accurately capture all the transactions going on in the business on a weekly and monthly basis. This information has to be accurate, timely, and complete or else the reports that come from it won't fully reflect what's really going on in the business. If you don't know how to find a great bookkeeper, ask your accountant.

- Have accurate and complete monthly and annual financials: Income Statement, Cash Flow Statement, and Balance Sheet.

- Be sure you have a personal Balance Sheet. Keep business and personal separate, though often the bank will look at both personal and business financials in order to make an informed decision about a loan. Include your resume so the bank can see your experience.

- Know the cash conversion cycle—the time lag between when the business pays the suppliers and when in turn it gets paid by customers.

- Know exactly why you are applying for a loan and how exactly do you intend to use the funds if the loan comes through. Be able to show how the loan will be paid back.

- Know the difference between financing working capital for a going concern and start-up capital for a business that has not reached going-concern status.

- Know what time of year the business will need cash from a credit line and apply for the line at least six months before the cash crunch hits. Reread the section called "Budgeting Cash the Easy Way" in Chapter 5 if you're stumped.

Now on to the don'ts.

Don'ts When Working with a Bank

- Don't fight with the bank if you owe it money. You will lose.

- Don't assume all loans are for "working capital." Some are for building inventory, paying payroll, etc. Be specific on what the loan's purpose is.

- Don't even think about approaching the bank without updated financial statements (Net Income Statements, Cash Flow Statements, and Balance Sheet). This will seriously damage your credibility and you might not get a second chance.

- Don't use tax returns as a substitute for monthly and annual financial statements. Tax returns only reveal what the business declares in income for tax purposes. It's not meaningful to a creditor like a bank.

- Don't present financial statements that are incomplete or inaccurate. Be sure your accountant checks them before you send them to the lender.

- Don't take on debt for the business and your personal life at the same time. The bank cares about both.

- Don't ask the bank to loan the business money because you will not do your job. (Got your attention with that one, didn't I?) Too many small business owners/managers would rather pay interest to the bank than pick up the phone and call customers who owe them money! The bank is not there to pick up your slack. Reread Chapter 6 to learn how to collect the money that is owed to your business.

* * *

Managing a small business is not for the faint of heart. There are seasons in a business when it makes perfect sense to take on debt to expand the customer base, hire crackerjack experts, or finance cash flow while waiting for customer payments. The Balance Sheet holds the key to whether the business you manage can comfortably take on more debt without putting the business at risk. If total assets are twice the size of total liabilities, the Balance Sheet is strong and owner's equity is positive. If current assets are twice the size of current liabilities, the business is probably liquid enough to handle its short-term cash needs. If assets are growing faster than liabilities, the net worth of the business is growing. The cumulative effect of managing the small business is bearing fruit.

In the next chapter, I'll put your entire financial dashboard together so you can drive the small business to grow profits, improve cash flow, and increase owner's equity. You already know more than most small business managers. Congratulations.

KEY TAKEAWAYS

▶ The Balance Sheet is the cumulative report for everything that has happened in the business until the present. It's the state of the business at a moment in time.

▶ The Balance Sheet is an indispensable statement on your financial dashboard. Nowhere else are all assets, liabilities, and owner's equity captured.

▶ A strong Balance Sheet is characterized as having a strong and liquid asset base that can comfortably cover liabilities (obligations of the business).

▶ As gross margin and cash flow improve, and total expenses stay below the breakeven point, the Balance Sheet gets stronger and owner's equity improves. Lenders always look favorably on businesses with strong Balance Sheets.

▶ If you are managing a small business, you must be able to print out the Net Income Statement, Cash Flow Statement, and Balance Sheet for the business every month and at the end of the year. A great bookkeeper can make this an easy task. Don't procrastinate.

▶ Borrowing money is not a bad thing. Well-run businesses use the cash from short- or long-term loans to build up their assets.

▶ Make the bank your partner. It cares about managing risk, but it also cares that the small business you manage succeeds. The loan process may look different at each lending institution, but the analytic process is very similar. Now it's not a mystery to you.

CHAPTER 9

Putting It All Together

Your Financial Dashboard in Real Time

When I was 16, I couldn't wait to get my driver's license. It was a rite of passage, the promise of adulthood and greater freedom. Never mind those horrible accident photos we were shown in driver's ed in an attempt to get us to recognize there was risk involved. That wasn't going to happen to me! I knew better. I wasn't foolish. I was responsible, and my level-headed nature would be enough to keep me safe. A few decades and one near-fatal car accident later, all my delusions had vanished. A small patch of black ice is all it took one frigid February afternoon to lose control of a few tons of heavy steel hurtling down the highway at 55 miles per hour.

After my accident, I knew I had to do something or risk losing my confidence behind the wheel, so I took a high-performance driving course. While my classmates wanted to learn how to cut turns at 90 miles an hour, I just wanted to learn how to survive in all road conditions.

My instructors were racecar drivers. Part of the curriculum was to take students out in a long-bed truck to a skid pad on the track. During the demonstration of the exercise, the instructor drove the truck in a tight circle at 40 miles an hour. The truck skidded all over the track, which was exactly what had happened with my car when I had the accident, just before impact—and the instructor showed us how to handle it.

The instructor saw I was shaken by the demonstration and asked me if I wanted to continue. I replied, "I want to skid out a thousand times and learn how to handle any kind of skid. I want to change my innate responses to a skid to avoid accidents in the future. I want my safe response to a skid to become second nature." So while everyone else was eating lunch, my instructor and I skidded on that infernal pad over and over until good reflexes finally kicked in, with the hope that if I ever did skid out again, I'd have a faster and more informed response.

Many entrepreneurs I've met feel about business as I initially did about driving. They see only the promise and none of the risks. Or if they do see the risks, they minimize them through faulty assumptions. But if you can read your financial dashboard, you are in a position to make better business decisions beforehand, no matter what the economic conditions.

What I've tried to do in the book is to help you manage the skids and risks when you run a small business. Norm Brodsky, veteran serial entrepreneur, author, and financial columnist, whom you'll meet in Chapter 10, estimates that more than half the businesses that go bankrupt in the United States do so because those running the business couldn't read the financial risks before they reached the point of no return.

I want to spare every small business manager reading this book that kind of agony. The same way my racecar instructor taught me the basics in the classroom before he took me out on the track, I've been instructing you in Chapters 1 through 8. You've been learning about each of the gauges of the financial dashboard, one by one and line by line, so that you can understand what each gauge or statement measures, and so that you know how to read them. I wanted you to maintain focus and to be able to take your time with each idea so it would make sense and stay with you.

I've kept you in the classroom—off the road, so to speak—to teach you how to interpret what your dashboard is telling you.

Now it's time to go out on the track, turn on the ignition, and see what happens when you turn the wheel, step on the gas, or tap the brake. Now it's time to see what happens to each statement on the financial dashboard as standard transactions take place.

BASIC BUSINESS TRANSACTIONS

There are really just a few types of recurring activities that drive a small business. While financial advisors make a princely living trying to convince you otherwise, the following transactions, with some slight variations, probably cover 75 percent what occurs when running a small business:

- You sell a product or a service for cash.

- You sell a product or service on payment terms.

- You collect on a receivable.

- You pay an expense with a check or on terms.

- You pay an expense with a credit card.

- You take out a loan.

- You pay back a loan.

Let's see what happens to your financial dashboard with each of these events.

Selling a Product or Service for Cash

When you sell a product or service, you receive cash or a cash equivalent, like a credit card, as payment. (Note: I'm not getting into discounts and credit card exchange fees right now. Let's keep things simple.)

What Happens on Your Net Income Statement

Net revenue increases by the value of the sale, COGS increases by the value of what it cost you to manufacture, purchase, or deliver that product or service, and gross margin increases too, by the difference between net revenue and COGS. Higher gross margin helps us breathe a little easier. If you're receiving at least a 45 percent premium over COGS, as we discussed in Chapters 2 and 3, then you're making money on every sale, which is what you want. What was that mantra again? *Every product or service must have a gross margin of at least 30 percent of net revenue or 45 percent above cost of goods sold.*

What Happens on Your Cash Flow Statement

When customers pay you cash, your cash position improves. Any time cash comes in or out of the business for any reason, that transaction will always get captured on the Cash Flow Statement as either Cash In or Cash Out. In this case, Cash In increases as soon as payment is made. The faster cash comes into the business, the easier it is for the business to pay its bills. Love that.

What Happens on Your Balance Sheet

The three lines that would probably change on the Balance Sheet as a result of this cash sale are cash (current asset), inventory (current asset), and potentially, owner's equity.

Cash is a current asset, so any time it changes on the Cash Flow Statement, it will also change on the Balance Sheet. If you manage a cash-based business, like selling ice cream, every sale is most likely a cash sale, so when net revenue increases, the cash balance increases on both the Cash Flow Statement and the Balance Sheet. Since you're making a positive gross margin (reflected on the Net Income Statement) each time you sell an ice cream cone, the Balance Sheet shows an increase in both current assets and owner's equity equal to the value of the gross margin on the sale.

Accounts receivable doesn't change because the item was paid for on the spot—happily the business manager doesn't have to worry about collecting outstanding invoices.

Another line that will reflect a change on the Balance Sheet is inventory. You remember from Chapter 6 that inventory is considered a current asset because it can be converted into cash within 12 months. Before a sale, the only place you'll see the value of that inventory is on the Balance Sheet under current assets on the inventory line, valued at what you paid for it, as COGS. As soon as some of that inventory is sold, however, inventory on the Balance Sheet decreases because the customer walked out with the product. Inventory decreases, but you sold that ice cream at a profit. If you can keep doing that—and the profit is at least COGS plus 45 percent—you'll build a going concern.

If you *buy* ice cream at COGS on payment terms and sell it right away for cash, your cash flow looks good. But what if it's the other way around? What if you have a product or service that you *sell* on payment terms?

Selling a Product or Service on Payment Terms

If you are a service provider, it's highly likely you provide the service and bill the customer to pay you at a later date. This transaction on the Net Income Statement looks similar to a cash transaction, but the Cash Flow Statement will not reflect the sale until the cash is collected on the invoice.

What Happens on Your Net Income Statement

The sale is captured on the Net Income Statement as net revenue whether the customer pays right away or a month from now. Both COGS and gross margin increase, just as they did on the cash sale. However, the business has to capture the fact that the client still has to pay this bill, which it does on the Balance Sheet. Remember, the Balance Sheet has an important role because it captures everything that's going on, both when the sale is made and when it's paid for.

What Happens on Your Cash Flow Statement

Nada! Zip! The Cash Flow Statement shows no activity because the business sold a product or a service that will be paid at a later time. No cash changed hands. The Cash Flow Statement is waiting patiently.

What Happens on Your Balance Sheet

The customer still owes the business payment for goods delivered or services rendered. This customer IOU is captured on the Balance Sheet as a current asset on the accounts receivable line, which increases by the value of the outstanding invoice. Inventory, also a current asset, decreases by the COGS value of the inventory that's been sold. Nowhere else on your financial dashboard can you see how much money is owed the business except on the Balance Sheet. The difference between the invoice value of the receivable and the COGS value of the inventory is the gross margin made on the sale. The value of that gross margin is reflected on the Balance Sheet under owner's equity.

Here's why *collecting on all your receivables* is so important. If you don't collect from your customers, the business is carrying the burden of paying for the COGS on the products shipped without any benefit of cash payment or increase in owner's equity. That's accelerating the business in the wrong direction!

Collecting on a Receivable

After reading Chapters 5 and 6, you understand that an invoice that has not been paid by a customer becomes a receivable to the business—and that collecting on your receivables is extremely important.

When Susie sends you payment on an outstanding receivable, it's usually in the form of a check or a wire transfer. If you have a choice, choose the wire transfer. You'll have access to the cash sooner than if you have to wait for a check to clear.

What Happens on Your Net Income Statement
Nothing changes on the Net Income Statement when you collect a receivable. The sale was already captured as net revenue when the sale was made, not when it's paid.

What Happens on Your Cash Flow Statement

As soon as the wire transfer arrives in your account or the check from Susie clears, Cash In and Ending Cash increase on the Cash Flow Statement. No surprise, but how nice that cash flow just improved. It's not that the number went up that's important here; what's important is that you have the cash to pay your expenses!

What Happens on Your Balance Sheet

On the Balance Sheet, the value of total current assets doesn't change because you just swapped out one current asset for another of equal value—an account receivable for cash. Now you have more cash to work with and your accounts receivable are smaller. The business becomes more liquid when there's more cash. This is what you want.

Paying an Expense with Cash or on Terms

Whenever you pay a bill, it's considered a cash transaction, whether you pay via check, wire transfer, or a greasy paper sack of crumpled dollar bills. This pertains to any bill, whether it's for a fixed expense, such as rent or insurance, or a variable expense, such as supplies, advertising, or raw materials.

Let's say the business paid the rent for the month. Here's what you'd see on your financial dashboard as soon as that transaction clears.

What Happens on Your Net Income Statement

When you pay a bill, it shows up as either a fixed or variable expense on the Net Income Statement. Fixed expenses are the same regardless of the volume of sales, whereas variable expenses tend to increase with changes in sales volume, as you may recall from Chapter 2. If your business uses the cash basis of accounting, this expense gets captured when it's paid. If your business uses the accrual basis of accounting (remember cash basis and accrual basis from Chapter 5?), this expense gets captured in the month the invoice is due.

What Happens on Your Cash Flow Statement

When you pay a bill, Cash Out increases and Ending Cash decreases. Simple as that. However, if the bill offers the option of paying in 30 days (instead of saying "due on receipt") and you choose to wait (as most of us do), the Cash Flow Statement does not change until the bill is paid.

I hope that this is all becoming second nature to you. In fact, if much of this chapter seems like old hat, I've done my job and you're well on your way to success.

What Happens on Your Balance Sheet

Stop! Read no further. Try to guess what happens here. Seriously, jot down what are by now your informed guesses. Done? Okay, now you can go on to the next paragraph.

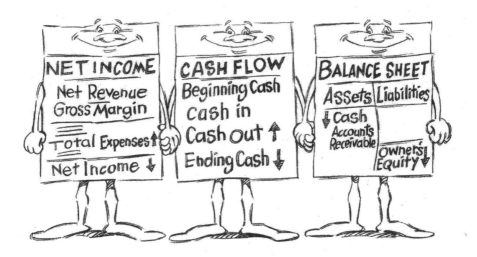

If the business pays a bill immediately, current assets decreases (on the cash line) by the amount of the invoice. If the business pays at some point in the future, usually 30 days, the invoice is captured as a current liability (on the accounts payable line), and so the total of your current liabilities increases by the amount of the invoice. Once that invoice is paid, a current liability (accounts payable) decreases and a current asset (cash) decreases by a corresponding amount. (Again, I'm avoiding any discussions on discounts or interest or late fees here.) The Balance Sheet balances—and owner's equity remains the same—because a current asset, in this case cash, has paid for a current liability, in this case an account payable.

Paying an Expense with a Credit Card

If you pay a bill using a credit card, you have incurred a current liability for the business. Instead of owing the supplier, for example, now you owe the credit card company. What really happened is that the credit card company paid the supplier on behalf of the business.

What Happens on Your Net Income Statement

Whether you're using the cash or accrual method of accounting, the Net Income Statement shows the fixed and variable expenses paid that month. If the credit card balance was not fully paid off, incurring interest charges on the balance owed, these additional charges show up under variable expenses on a separate line called "Interest Expense."

Credit cards are used for many types of expenses, such as marketing (business lunches), entertaining, and travel expenses, and these expenses are broken out as separate line items showing each one has been paid. This is actually quite useful, as it forces you to take note of how you are using your credit card, since there is no single line item for "credit card expense."

What Happens on Your Cash Flow Statement

When you purchase a product or service with credit, nothing changed on the cash flow statement because no cash was involved. A short-term loan was extended by the credit card company to the business. When the credit card bill gets paid, however, Cash Out increases, reducing Ending Cash. The Cash Flow Statement also has line items that capture what was paid and when it was paid. That too makes it easy to keep track of actual Cash Out and helps you build your cash flow budget for the future.

What Happens on Your Balance Sheet

The actual balance owed on the credit card or credit line shows up on the Balance Sheet under current liabilities on the "credit line payable" line. It is considered a short-term loan that is outstanding. My personal bias is that credit card bills should be paid in full monthly. Others may disagree, but I've found that it's one of the most important ways to prevent debt problems from arising.

When the credit card bill is actually paid, the credit line payable under current liabilities decreases, and a current asset, cash, decreases by the same amount. The Balance Sheet stays balanced—and owner's equity remains the same.

The biggest trap I've seen small business managers get into is growing current liabilities on credit cards too large or too fast. Either they can't pay the balance off or they pay only the minimum monthly payment. The risk grows of never paying off the balance due to high interest fees that can mushroom quickly. Remember that poor fellow from Chapter 7, the one with $400,000 due on the business's five credit cards? Don't let his plight become your own. A word to the wise: Don't ever let current liabilities, what the business owes, grow larger than current assets. If you manage the business with this advice in mind, you'll reap the dual benefit of protecting your sanity and keeping the business solvent.

And one last word on paying with credit: If there is an increase in current liabilities without an equal increase in assets, owner's equity decreases. Bad idea! The net worth of the business has eroded. This may occasionally be okay in the short term, but you want this downward trend in owner's equity to reverse as quickly as possible. The section entitled "How to Improve Your Balance Sheet" in Chapter 8 took you through how to do this.

Taking Out a Loan

A credit card or a credit line is a short-term liability. If you have a credit line with the bank, it's possible to use the cash proceeds from that loan for many reasons. The bank might place some constraints, but typically, a credit line is used for paying suppliers, buying raw materials, and financing the time lag between when a sale is made and when the client pays the invoice. The business still has bills to pay as it waits for client payment, so that's called "financing the accounts receivable gap." Until you use the cash for one purpose or another, little changes on your dashboard.

What Happens on Your Net Income Statement

Nothing changes on the Net Income Statement until either the interest payment is due or you pay the interest on the loan. When you pay the interest, it shows up as interest expense. Repayment of the principle is not viewed as an expense and therefore does not show up (you have to go to the Balance Sheet for that).

What Happens on Your Cash Flow Statement

The Cash Flow Statement captures the inflow of cash you've drawn down from the credit line as an increase in Cash In. Ending Cash will increase as well, unless and until it gets spent—hopefully on necessities, not luxuries.

What Happens on Your Balance Sheet

The Balance Sheet captures both the inflow of cash under current assets as well as the outstanding current liability of the credit line that must be paid back to the bank. Since assets and liabilities both increase by the same amount, there is no change to owner's equity. If the bank extends a credit line and it isn't used, you don't have a liability. There's nothing to pay back. The moment you use part or all of an available credit line, it gets captured as a current liability (under credit line payable) on the Balance Sheet.

Here's the deal. When you take out debt, make sure the cash proceeds are invested in something that will increase revenues, improve productivity (lower the COGS), or decrease expenses. That way, the cash from the credit line has the potential to improve the profitability and cash flow of the business. Read the last two sentences carefully. This single piece of advice is worth the entire price of this book.

Paying Back a Loan

A loan has two parts, the **interest** (the amount charged by the lender to the borrower for the use of the money) and the **principal** (the original value of the loan or what remains of it as you pay it off). Let's assume a monthly transaction where you pay both interest and principal on a long-term loan, for example, a mortgage. Here's what happens on the financial dashboard.

What Happens on Your Net Income Statement
The Net Income Statement captures the interest payment as a variable expense, as it does all interest payments whether the loan is a short-term (current) or a long-term liability. The repayment of principal will not be captured on the Net Income Statement because it's not viewed as an expense, but merely a repayment of debt. Net income will decrease for the period as the interest expense is realized and you'll see that reflected on the Net Income Statement.

What Happens on Your Cash Flow Statement
The Cash Flow Statement will capture the decrease in cash due to payment of interest as well as principle. Cash Out will increase, and Ending Cash will decrease.

What Happens on Your Balance Sheet
As the principal gets paid off, the Balance Sheet will capture the decrease in cash under current assets as well as the equivalent decrease in the amount of debt outstanding under long-term liabilities.

If the loan has been used to purchase a building that improved in value, cash decreases, but fixed assets might very well increase depending on what happens to the value of real estate. If the loan has been used to build inventory, then again, cash decreases while inventory increases. What the loan was used for—and whether that asset increases or decreases in value over time—determines whether owner's equity increases or decreases.

Now that you can anticipate the outcomes of typical day-to-day business transactions , you're ready to leave the track and start driving on the expressway. Before you do, however, there are key ratios you need to know that will act like a high-tech GPS system. They'll orient you on the journey so you'll know when to make course corrections.

RATIOS AND PERCENTAGES HELP FIND THE PATTERNS

It's important to be able to track the numbers as transactions happen, which I just did for you above. The larger goal, however, is to be able to see patterns in the business and anticipate what they mean for the future.

Ratios and percentages will help you see how the numbers relate to each other. It's not enough to track how key measures are increasing or decreasing, but how they are doing relative to other measures. Accountants call these comparisons "ratios." Ratios are simple fractions, as you'll see in a moment, but like any fraction, you can also express the fraction as a percent. Accounting convention presents certain ratios—net margin and gross margin—as percentages, while others—current ratio and quick ratio—remain simple ratios. Whether you think of them as ratios or percentages, they allow you to compare the performance of the business from one period to another. They help you see what is improving and what is having problems before the crisis hits. If you keep track of the ratios and percentages listed here, you'll be in ship shape.

Net Margin Percentage

The **net margin percentage** shows the relationship between your net revenue and your true (net) profit. It expresses the relationship between the top and bottom lines on your Net Income Statement.

$$\text{Net Margin Percentage} =$$
$$\text{Net Income} \div \text{Net Revenue} \times 100$$

This is an efficiency ratio. It measures the portion of every dollar of net revenue that becomes net profit for that period. If your net margin percentage is improving, it means more of your net revenues drop to your bottom line. That's what you want. Changes in this percentage show whether the profit percentage is improving or degrading. Track it from month to month to check on the direction of its change. Also, it's important that you know what profit percentages are in your industry. If your profit percentages are higher than your industry's average, you're on the right track. If not, you need to improve gross margin (by charging more or reducing COGS) or reduce operating expenses.

You'll find net revenue and net income on the Net Income Statement.

Gross Margin Percentage

Gross margin equals your net revenue minus the cost of goods sold (I know, I know. I'm really putting you to sleep here). The **gross margin percentage** shows you what percentage of every net revenue dollar is gross margin—that is, profit before expenses. This is important to know because gross margin is the money that pays all the business's bills.

$$\text{Gross Margin Percentage} = \text{Gross Margin} \div \text{Net Revenue} \times 100$$

You learned in Chapters 2 and 3 that 30 percent is the goal, that is, 30 cents on every dollar of sales should be gross margin if the business can be expected to survive. Again, each industry has its norms for gross margin percentage and you should know what it is in your industry; 30 percent is merely a benchmark.

You'll also find net revenue and gross margin on the Net Income Statement.

Accounts Receivable Turnover Rate

The **accounts receivable turnover rate** is a measure of the efficiency of your collections department (is that you? your bookkeeper? your mother-in-law?). It is found on the "days receivable report," which your bookkeeper or accountant can create for you, and it tells you how many times a year you collect all your accounts receivable.

$$\text{Accounts Receivable Turnover Rate} =$$
$$\text{Yearly Credit Sales} \div \text{Accounts Receivable}$$

Credit sales are sales transactions where the client receives the good or service and is extended payment terms to pay the bill with cash or a cash equivalent at some point in the future. In this equation we are using the total amount of credit sales throughout the year.

Hopefully, the number on that report comes close to 12. That means you're collecting on your receivables every month. The smaller the number, the longer it's taking you to collect on accounts receivable—and the worse for your business.

But be careful: Since this is an average, some seriously "aged" accounts may be hidden there. You're probably better off looking at that monthly aging invoices report I suggested you have your bookkeeper generate for you, back in Chapter 6.

Current Ratio

Your **current ratio** is a measure of short-term liquidity. It's found by looking at total current assets and total current liabilities on your Balance Sheet and will tell you if there's enough liquidity in the business to pay short-term obligations.

Current Ratio =
Total Current Assets ÷ Total Current Liabilities

Total current assets include cash, accounts receivable, and inventory. Just divide total current assets by total current liabilities and you'll get your current ratio. A ratio of 2:1 will pretty much guarantee sleep-filled nights for you, and stress-free days for your bookkeeper.

Quick Ratio

The **quick ratio** is a variation on the current ratio presented above, but it removes the value of inventory from current assets. That makes it a more conservative estimate of how much liquidity is in the business. (Sometimes inventory is hard to liquidate, so this ratio has backed out the value of inventory from total current assets.)

Quick Ratio =
(Cash + Accounts Receivable) ÷ Total Current Liabilities

You'll always find cash, accounts receivable, and current liabilities on the Balance Sheet. These current accounts provide a sharp focus on how much cash and cash equivalents are available at a given moment to pay total current liabilities if payment is required right now. You always want this ratio to be 1:1 at a minimum.

Ideally, you want current assets to exceed current liabilities in case the bank or a supplier demands payment immediately, which can happen in tough markets.

As the business grows, there are other ratios to keep an eye on, but the ones listed above provide a great foundation for managing a small business. If you watch these on a monthly basis, you're so far ahead of your peers, they'll be eating your dust.

* * *

So there you have the financial dashboard in motion, and a GPS system to help get you where you want to go. You should always start with the Net Income Statement because that's where net revenues are captured and all the expenses associated with generating them and with running the business.

Then you look at the Cash Flow Statement to see what has changed there, because keeping tabs on ending cash is crucial when you're trying to build a going concern and avoid bankruptcy. The Balance Sheet always comes last because it takes numbers from the other two statements and integrates the cumulative effects of all transactions from the day the business was born.

Standard accounting software will calculate these ratios with a few clicks of the mouse. You can have your bookkeeper show you how, or even ask that these ratios be included on the regular financial reports he or she generates.

What I learned on that racetrack was that a skid didn't have to end in a near-fatal crash; learning how to steer made all the difference. Now you know how to steer your business.

KEY TAKEAWAYS

Daily

► Check your cash balances daily to compare how much cash you have against the cash you'll need. (You learned to capture your "needs" by making a cash flow budget in Chapter 6.) An online bank account will make checking cash balances and paying bills electronically that much faster and easier.

► Deposit checks immediately so you have access to the cash as soon as possible. Out-of-town checks take that much longer to clear. If any check bounces, you'll learn that sooner too.

▶ Use the information from the "aging invoices report" that your bookkeeper has generated at your request to put collection calls on your calendar. Make those calls part of your daily routine before their bills come due. (Chapter 6 showed you easy ways to do this.)

Weekly

▶ Have your accountant or bookkeeper create a Cash Flow Statement for your review every week.

▶ Compare your weekly Cash Flow Statement against your cash flow budget and make adjustments for the following week based on what has changed.

▶ Review all the payments customers made that week and make note of the late payers. That will help you determine if you still want to service those clients or change the payment terms.

▶ If you have someone, like an accounts payable clerk, paying bills on behalf of the business, make sure you review those checks with their corresponding invoices for every payment over $250 before the checks go out. It keeps everyone accountable.

Monthly

▶ Have your accountant or bookkeeper create a Net Income Statement and Balance Sheet for your review every month.

▶ Look at the key ratios and percentages we discussed in this chapter and see how they've changed. If they've improved, great. If they've started to slip, put a simple plan together to help improve them next month. Every chapter in this book gives you tips on how to do that.

▶ Review your credit card statements every month to make sure every charge listed is legitimate. If you catch a problem quickly, there's a higher likelihood you'll get better support from the credit card issuer to help resolve it in your favor.

CHAPTER **10**

Numbers Make the Business

An Interview with Norm Brodsky

Norm Brodsky, "Street Smarts" columnist and senior contributing editor for *Inc.* magazine, has experienced the heights and the depths of what it means to run a small business. Among the six businesses he has founded and grown is Citistorage, a document-archive company, which he built to a mega-million-dollar success before selling it in 2007 for $110 million. He has declared bankruptcy twice in his life.

Citistorage began as a messenger business. When one client asked Norm to store four boxes, it changed the course of the company's history. Now, if you visit Williamsburg, Brooklyn, you'll see great white and blue industrial buildings that stretch whole city blocks storing millions of boxes. Citistorage was a big part of the gentrification of Williamsburg, proof that successful businesses can change neighborhoods and lives. Norm, his wife Elaine, and their executive team built a corporate culture that was the envy of every Fortune 500 company.

I used to bring my students to visit the company so they could be inspired by a brilliantly run organization. It's one thing to talk about great management in the classroom, it's quite another to see it in action. The Brodskys are not only great corporate citizens, they're wonderful neighbors to the community. The company contributes mountains of gifts for needy families during the holidays and is famous for the annual Fourth of July block party, when thousands of people come to the waterfront to experience Norm's generosity firsthand.

As generous as he is, Norm is no softy. The staff gave Norm the nickname "Stormin' Norman" for a reason; when he has a vision, nothing can stop him. Norm is a serial entrepreneur with a passion to help small businesses thrive. He's given thousands of talks about what it takes to run a successful company and personally mentored hundreds of entrepreneurs. He is also a well-respected author and philanthropist. This self-made man now shares with you what he learned on his journey. The great news is, everything Norm talks about you have read in this book.

INSIDE THE MIND OF NORM BRODSKY

I was lucky enough to have several hours with Norm. I can't think of anything better to leave you with than a partial transcript of our time together.

> **Dawn:** *Norm, thanks for your time today. I appreciate the opportunity to share this interview in a book I'm writing, designed to help small businesses, many of which are hurting.*

Norm: That's everybody! I've seen a lot of businesses that went bankrupt that could have made it. They have a great idea, product, or service, they have the selling skills—but they run out of cash. The owners are stunned when it happens. Most people say, "I didn't have enough money. I ran out of money." It's not that they didn't have enough money; they didn't use the money properly. It's a basic thing. The way they normally learn is by trial and error or luck. Most of the small businesses that fail do so because the entrepreneur doesn't have a general understanding of the numbers of the business. My philosophy is that numbers make the business. They are not hard to understand. You don't have to be schooled in accounting. I was an accounting major in college and I didn't get it because I didn't want to get it. I was sales driven. If you have an understanding of these critical numbers you can see trouble coming.

The Financial Dashboard Is the Key to Small Business Survival

Dawn: *Why do you think so few small businesses survive?*

Norm: Knowing how to read your financial dashboard is the key to survival. In my experience, 90 percent of people who start a small business have no clue how to read their financials. That's why most don't survive. Most small business managers think it's complicated, so they're afraid of it. It's really easy to teach people how to monitor what drives their business success.

Dawn: *What's the first objective when you're running a small business?*

Norm: At the beginning the goal is survival. It has nothing to do with making or losing money. It's whether you can live off your own cash flow. That's the important part. Once the business is growing, there's lot of other things you can do.

Dawn: *How did you learn the numbers?*

Norm: My father taught me. He was a door-to-door peddler before the advent of credit cards and department stores. I asked him, "How do you make money?" He said, "It's really simple; you see this bottle here? You buy it for $1 and you sell it for $2. You have a 50 percent gross margin." I also learned the hard way. Even though I've been successful, I've gone bankrupt twice; once when I was 33 and the second time when I was 46. You can hire someone to do the accounting work, but you can't hire someone to understand your numbers. That's your job as an entrepreneur.

Dawn: *Why do you think most entrepreneurs don't know how to read a basic financial statement?*

Norm: Because most entrepreneurs started in sales. They think sales are the only thing that drives the business and determines success. It's important, but there's a lot more to running a successful business. Every time I speak to large groups, I always ask the same question. "How many of you started your careers in sales and now run your own small business?" An overwhelming majority, usually over half the audience, raises their hands. What do salespeople know about running a business? All they know is sales. They think, "I sold a million dollars for this other company, I can do it for myself." They probably can.

But what they don't understand is what goes into a business besides sales. Just because you're good at sales doesn't mean you won't go bankrupt.

Dawn: *Why wouldn't hiring an accountant be the answer?*

Norm: One of the most important things I do is to counsel people on the lingo their financial people and accountants use so at least they know the basics. Accountants, though, are historians. Their function is important because the past informs the future. But by the time you get the numbers from the accountant, it's too late. While you can learn a lot from history, you can't survive on history, you have to survive on the present. You need to have a basic understanding of how to measure what drives the business. You could go back to school and take accounting classes. But even if you do, it takes a long time. The courses are also in such depth I'm not sure they teach the basic ABCs of running a business. The other problem is, you could take an accounting course, pass it, and still not understand how to run a business.

Dawn: *What few basic things does every small business manager need to know?*

Norm: I think the most important statement is the Cash Flow Statement. You need to understand what it is, how it works, and what it tells you. If you don't have enough cash to pay your bills, you're out of business. You can't buy your product because you can't pay your suppliers and you can't pay your people. When I mentor small business owners we review revenues, costs, cash flow, and budgeting. I run through hundreds of flip charts going through this stuff! How many people know a prof-

itable business could be going bankrupt? Entrepreneurs need to understand the difference between cash flow and profits. Most don't. So here's a question for you, when is a sale complete?

Dawn: *When you collect on that sale.*

Norm: That's right! If you're not a candy store, you don't collect right away. Your sales plan might be great, but you could still run out of money! Entrepreneurs will say, "Whattya mean I'm gonna run outta money?" They don't understand if they plan to do $5K a month in sales and they only do $4K, that could bankrupt them. Your day-to-day operations start on a cash basis. You have limited cash. You have to make sure you don't run out of it. Whether you're making money or not is captured on the Net Income Statement, but that has nothing to do with cash flow. They have to understand the difference. Cash is the hardest thing to replenish and the easiest thing to lose.

Mistakes Every Entrepreneur Makes

Dawn: *What recurring problems do you see?*

Norm: Every entrepreneur I have ever met makes the same two mistakes: They overestimate sales and they underestimate the cost to run the business. How do I know? I made the same mistakes. The first thing I teach people is to be realistic with what they can do in sales. They're fooling themselves when they're too aggressive. Sales and collections drive cash flow, so if sales projections are unrealistic, cash flow will be off. If they don't have enough cash, they're out of business. I see these crazy sales estimates and I say, "These projections are not achievable!" They say they're constrained because they can only raise $200K so they increase the sales expectations to make up the shortfall. Not a good strategy. They should scale the business according to how much start-up capital they have and be conservative. See what the business can actually generate in sales and what it will actually cost. Most buy a computer program and arbitrarily estimate sales and expenses based on available capital, not what the market is telling them. Projections are not for investors; they're designed to help you run the business. If your projections are not realistic you're destined to fail from the beginning.

Dawn: *How do entrepreneurs project what they need to start a business?*

Norm: They have no idea how much money they need to start a business. The overwhelming majority don't go to business school. They might be able to project net revenue and net income but they have no clue about cash flow projections. They don't understand what the relationship is between one number and another number.

I mentor 20 small business owners a month pro bono. They all have the same problem. When I ask them to do a cash flow statement they hand me what they think is a cash flow statement.

They'll say, "Here are my sales projections, here's what it's going to cost me, and here's how much money I'm going to make." That's very nice, but they'll go broke before they get there. Why? Because they only budget their expected profits, not their expected cash flow.

In a start-up business, you can be losing money and still stay in business if you manage your cash flow right. Most people don't get that because they don't know the difference between cash and accrual accounting. Showing a profit on the Net Income Statement doesn't tell you if you have enough cash to achieve that bottom line.

Accounting on a cash basis is typical for small businesses that generate less than $5 million in annual sales. It captures cash transactions as they happen. Accrual accounting, however, helps manage the timing of cash flow for receivables and payables in the future. When a sale is made and when the business gets paid for it has to be tracked. It's the only way to know if you'll have enough cash to run the business now and in the future, week by week, month by month.

The Real Reasons Entrepreneurs
Run Out of Money

Dawn: Most entrepreneurs say they went bankrupt because they didn't have enough start-up capital.

Norm: In almost every case, they don't understand how to use the start-up money they do have. One of the most common mistakes when people open a business is to rent an office and buy fancy furniture. Entrepreneurs have got to understand that the money they get from their first round, whether it's their own money or from family or a friend, is easy to raise. But once that money is spent, they can't go back twice to those people. The bank won't loan them money until they're a going concern so that's not an option. They have nowhere else to go. The use of that money is their lifeline; if they run out of that lifeline, they won't succeed.

Dawn: So most entrepreneurs don't understand the difference between luxuries and necessities?

Norm: Exactly. When cash is tight at the beginning—and it always is—a lot of entrepreneurs spend money on luxuries. They don't get that. It's a luxury to have anything that doesn't directly help generate cash flow. Remember, cash is the hardest commodity to get and the easiest commodity to spend. You can't replenish it easily.

Dawn: How did you decide what to cut when cash was tight?

Norm: When I was 33 and went broke, I sat down with my wife. We had to figure out how much money we had to live on for the next 12 months. We also had to figure out where we could cut back. In my mind, we had to get rid of one of the cars. She said, "We need two cars! We have different schedules." I said, "Having two cars is a luxury. We're going to have to plan our lives better. It's a necessity we have a car, it's not a necessity we have two cars." If you're going to conserve cash at the beginning, you have to be brutal about cutting expenses to a bare minimum.

Dawn: You've clearly seen this dynamic with other small businesses.

Norm: There was one great software business that had so much potential; instead, it went bankrupt. They came to me after the fact. I asked, "What did you do with all the start-up money?" Their offices, logo, and stationery were gorgeous. Everything was high-end. So these software guys spent a fortune on an office no client would ever see because they work on-site at their clients. I said, "You spent all that money on luxuries." They disagreed with me even after they went through Chapter 11!

I was in business 20 years before I bought a piece of new furniture because it was a luxury. Now I have opulent offices. When I was starting out, it was a necessity to have a chair. But I didn't need a designer chair with an automatic massage thing in it. Why do I need fancy stuff?

The Numbers That Drive the Business Matter Most

Dawn: The numbers can be daunting because there are so many! How do you stay focused?

Norm: Every business has certain numbers that reveal trends and the future health of the business. Here's where history is useful, especially for businesses that have been in operation for a while. A restaurant owner, for example, can tell you what his cash flow numbers are going to look like next week based on how many seats are filled on a Saturday night.

Every business has different, key measures that show patterns of opportunity and risk. When I owned the storage business, I could tell we had a problem based on certain numbers I would watch weekly. These included what we did in net revenues, how many deliveries we did, how many boxes we put away, and who owed us money and how much.

I got so good at looking at these indicators that I could tell my accountant how much money we made before he pulled the reports.

Dawn: *One of the indicators you look at is accounts receivable.*

Norm: If you sell on terms, part of that net revenue is not going to be collected, ever. I've been in business long enough to know, maybe 96–98 percent of receivables are collectible. It's important to understand that for planning and projections. No business that sells its products or services on terms collects 100 percent of outstanding invoices. You must have an allowance for bad debt when you make cash flow projections.

Dawn: *How do you manage accounts receivable?*

Norm: You have a list. You go down that list to remind clients to pay their bills one day after their bill was due. Most small business managers wait until they run out of cash, then they realize a 30-day invoice is now 120 days old! By the time you get to that, you're in trouble. If a 30-day invoice isn't paid for 120 days, chances are, the client's not paying because they're in financial trouble.

How an Expert Collects Receivables

Dawn: *What advice do you have about managing accounts receivable?*

Norm: Small business managers don't understand how important it is to collect a receivable. If a client hasn't paid a 30-day invoice, the business should be calling that client on the 31st day. Jump on it. The customers who you've extended 90-day terms to who haven't paid their bill should be called on the 91st day. Even small businesses that have been in business for years don't follow this discipline. Don't let the receivable age. When customers owe you money, you're the bank!

Dawn: *What do small business managers normally do?*

Norm: Usually they let receivables slide until they realize they can't pay their bills. Then they check to see who owes them money. Then they have an "OMG" moment. One guy owes them $100,000, he's 120 days overdue and he should have paid in 30 days! Then the bigger question is, why did you extend this customer that kind of credit in the first place? The business won't survive without receiving customer payments on time. Talk about payment terms up front when you're having the sales conversation. Once the sale is made, you have to track delivery of the service as well as the receivable for payment.

Dawn: *How do you bring up payment terms as part of the sales conversation?*

Norm: Instead of chasing non-paying customers after the fact, wouldn't it be better to assess that risk up front and decide if you even want to accept that sale? We tell our clients, "We're glad to have your business. These are our payment terms. If you don't pay us in 30 days, we'll charge you 2 percent of the outstanding invoice." You don't become successful just chasing any sale.

Dawn: *How do you handle customers who want 60- or 90-day payment terms?*

Norm: The truth is, customers don't like to pay bills, especially the smaller businesses. You have the option of negotiating payment terms up front by saying "We can't afford to wait 60 days" or "We can't afford to fulfill the next order until we receive payment." If we extend a non-paying client more goods and services before they pay us what's outstanding, our risk is greater. That's how small businesses get in trouble. Whatever you do, don't keep doing work for a non-paying customer! Start calling overdue accounts weekly. Don't wait for a cash crisis to hit.

Discuss Payment Terms
During the Sales Conversation

Dawn: *What's the risk if payment terms are not discussed during the sales conversation?*

Norm: You make a sale. You say to the customer, company policy is payment is due in 30 days. The customer counteroffers to pay in 90 days. Now you have to make a decision. You can stand firm on the 30-day payment terms and walk away from the deal or accept the deal on his payment terms and decide if it's worth it. Here's how I think about that decision.

If the margins are really high, I'll consider it. If not, the business will be stronger if I walk away from the deal. Net revenues won't look as strong, but cash flow will be better.

Let's say the sale is for $1,000,000 with a gross margin of 24 percent or $240,000. If normal payment terms are 30 days, we would normally be financing an $80,000 receivable. This is assuming we get full payment at the end of the month. *[Norm rattled this off without a hitch. He had taken the gross margin ($240,000) and divided it by the 3 months it would be outstanding or $80,000 per month. I confess I was impressed.]* But the client wants an extra two months to pay, that is an additional $160,000 in accounts receivable the business has to carry. If the cost of carrying that additional $160,000 receivable is 60 percent, I need to know, does the business have an extra $100,000 to carry that sale? *[Sixty percent is Norm's cost of capital, a number this long-time businessman knows by heart. Your accountant can tell you what this number is for you.]* If not, this one sale could put me out of business even though net revenue looks great! Nobody thinks this way. Most entrepreneurs would not walk away from a million-dollar sale. But I would if I knew it would bankrupt me because the payment terms were too far out.

I'm not telling you to turn down the sale, you just need to know that if you accept that sale, you might have to borrow from the bank, or sell a receivable at a discount to raise cash to finance the receivable. You might be able to finance your receivables, you have a lot more options once the business is up and running and proven. You have to survive to do that. Making a sale on terms always involves risk. If you can measure that risk, you make a more intelligent decision.

Dawn: *You have to know what your costs are to do that analysis.*

Norm: Yes, but beyond that, you have to know the business has that additional $100K of cash flow to finance that receivable. There are other costs we didn't even talk about like allocating fixed overhead and accounting for sales commissions, which can be sizable.

Dawn: It's not just customers, but your salespeople need to be on board with the company's payment terms.

Norm: Exactly. We incent our salespeople to care about payment terms because that protects our cash flow. So making the sale is just the first step but they need to care about payment terms as well. My salespeople would come back to the office declaring "We made the sale!" My next question was always "When are we getting paid?" They almost never had an answer. Most salesmen sell the lowest-price items or services because they don't care about the gross margin on the sale or the payment terms. You've got to *make* them care.

At one point, when times got tough and payment dragged, we changed our internal sales commissions policy. We didn't pay sales commissions until the company gets paid. That sure guaranteed that they would have the conversation about payment terms with every client.

Negotiate payment terms during the initial sales conversation. Determine if the business can afford to carry that receivable. Make sure the receivable is followed up on a timely basis. That's how it should work.

Dawn: What do you say to customers who pay late?

Norm: It's simple. We say, "Listen, you made the commitment, you knew the condition of the sale, can we pick up the check? " Or "I'm just asking you to keep your promise."

Dawn: *Sometimes cash flow is tight even if you make the collections calls. What would you recommend?*

Norm: Most small business managers see their bills are due and if cash is tight, they duck collections calls or they send partial payment to one vendor or another. What they should do is call up the supplier before the invoice is due, be honest, and say something like, "We had trouble collecting our receivables, in the next 30 days we'll pay what we promised you." Then do it. It's always easy to make a deal with a supplier before the fact instead of after the fact.

Dawn: *What risks should we look out for when cash dries up?*

Norm: When small businesses run out of cash, the managers often don't pay their withholding tax. This is a really bad idea. It's the most expensive money because the fines are huge. And you can really get into trouble. If a small business doesn't pay payroll through a payroll system, the owner becomes personally liable for tax withholding. If entrepreneurs don't pay withholding taxes correctly, criminal charges could be raised. It's easy to conserve cash by not sending the IRS a check when cash is tight, but the risks are enormous. Whatever you do, pay your withholding taxes!

How a Successful Entrepreneur
Looks at a Balance Sheet

Dawn: *Why is the Balance Sheet important?*

Norm: How many people understand what a Balance Sheet is? Almost no one. When I look at a Balance Sheet, I focus on just two important numbers: current assets and current liabilities. If your current liabilities are greater than your current assets you're bankrupt, or you will be very shortly. It means you don't have enough cash or cash equivalents to cover short-term obligations.

Here's an example of a business that came to me when it was in trouble. I said they were bankrupt and they didn't believe me, so I took a look at their Balance Sheet. They had a bank loan that was due in three months for half a million dollars and current assets of a hundred thousand. They said, "The bank will give us an extension." Maybe they will, maybe they won't. I'm not saying they'll go out of business but I am saying that's a problem. It may not be a problem today, but when current liabilities are greater than current assets, you need to address it.

These entrepreneurs never looked at their Balance Sheet. They knew how to read the Net Income Statement and they were showing a profit, but they were still in perilous trouble. Suppliers aren't going to get paid on time and it will become more and more difficult to pay the bills. I could see it. They couldn't.

Dawn: How should entrepreneurs think about the Balance Sheet for planning purposes?

Norm: Managing your Balance Sheet and how much debt to take on should be part of completing annual budgets. Most businesses forecast net revenue and net income for the coming year, right? You need to keep track of the relationship between current assets and current liabilities too and work on that ratio if it's out of whack. Sure your suppliers might wait another 60 days. But wouldn't it be better if you had this in compliance so you didn't have to worry about it? You wouldn't have to take 400 collections calls either. Why not make your life easier?

How to Steer out of a Skid

Dawn: Norm, so many entrepreneurs come to you when they're in crisis. How do you approach them?

Norm: The first thing you have to do is straighten out the mess, then figure out *why* it happened in the first place. If you don't deal with why it happened, it's going to recur. I call that Groundhog Day Syndrome. You'll find they don't understand the basic numbers of the business so they don't know where they stand. They don't have to become accountants, but reading their financial dashboard is step one. Until you teach them that, nothing can get solved long term. I actually have them write their budgets by hand in pencil so they know exactly where the numbers come from. No Excel software allowed!

Often, an entrepreneur comes to me with a cash flow problem. We can straighten that out. They need to check their sales figures and they need to start collecting their receivables on time. I teach them how to handle creditors and vendors. But that's only solving the problems that occurred.

They need to know the day-to-day operations of the business to prevent these problems in the future. They need to feel comfortable tracking key indicators such as sales, gross margin, profit, and collections. They need to know where to find this information and how to interpret it.

Dawn: This is a lot to know! What information is not as important?

Norm: They don't have to understand the more complicated parts of the Balance Sheet, for example, retained earnings, common stock, and preferred stock. But the daily drivers of the business need to become intuitive. It's not difficult. Most entrepreneurs can learn what they need to know in a couple of hours. It's not an age thing either. I speak to young people starting businesses in college and they don't get it. It's hard enough to start a business. So many things are outside of your control, why not understand the things that are in your control? It'll increase your chances of survival if you can read and interpret your financial dashboard.

* * *

Norm's absolutely right. Learning to interpret your financial dashboard isn't hard, but it's crucial to business success.

KEY TAKEAWAYS

▶ Know how to read your financial dashboard. If you're an entrepreneur, it's your job.

▶ Know the difference between cash and accrual accounting. You need to see the full picture.

▶ Don't chase net revenue without knowing if the business will get paid.

▶ Understand how to negotiate for payment terms and how to collect on accounts receivable.

▶ Payment terms should be part of the sales conversation, not an afterthought.

▶ The Cash Flow Statement is king. It's the lifeblood of the business. Know it cold.

▶ The Balance Sheet current accounts will reveal if the financials are getting stronger or weaker.

▶ Don't try to skirt the IRS. It's a very costly strategy.

* * *

Congratulations on surviving *Accounting for the Numberphobic: A Survival Guide for Small Business Owners.* According to Norm Brodsky, over 90 percent of entrepreneurs don't know what's tucked between these chapters, but now *you* do. The probability of success for the small business you manage or the one that's been on your mind for years has just improved dramatically. You've learned how to avoid a lot of the potholes and ravines along the road to success.

The big mission of this book is to unleash the creativity and genius of talented people through viable businesses that grow profitably. When businesses survive and flourish, individuals, households, and communities thrive too. I've seen it with thousands of small business owners who were once struggling and now have found their way. They learned the ideas I've shared with you here. May you join their community too, dear reader.

GLOSSARY

accounts payable A current liability account on the Balance Sheet that typically captures outstanding invoices suppliers have sent the business for goods that have been shipped or services that have been rendered for the business. Also called *payables*.

accounts receivable A current asset account on the Balance Sheet that typically captures outstanding invoices that your business sends to customers after it ships merchandise or fulfills a service. Also called *receivables*.

accounts receivable turnover rate A measure of the efficiency of your collections department, indicating how many times a year it collects on receivables.

Accounts Receivable Turnover Rate =
Yearly Credit Sales ÷ Accounts Receivables

accrual basis accounting A method of accounting that captures sales and expenses *as they happen* regardless of when the cash event occurs; net revenues are booked when the goods are shipped out the door or invoices sent, not when payment is received and, similarly, expenses are booked when bills and invoices from suppliers or sub-contractors are due, not when the business pays them.

aging invoices report A report that shows all unpaid invoices, the due date for payment of each and the number of days it is outstanding, the amount due on each invoice, and the client responsible for each invoice.

assets What the business owns and has title to, including unpaid invoices.

B

Balance Sheet The financial statement that captures all the outstanding loans and debt or liabilities incurred by the business since its inception, the value of all your business's assets, and its net worth.

Beginning Cash The amount of money in a business's account at the beginning of the month, before payments are received and expenses paid; it's the same amount as the previous month's Ending Cash.

bond A usually long-term debt instrument that formalizes a loan between a lender and a borrower, reflecting the amount owed and payment terms for that specific loan; it's an asset (receivable) to the lender and a liability (payable) to the borrower.

bottom line See *net income.*

breakeven point The point at which a business "breaks even," which occurs when its net income is neither positive nor negative but is *zero*, net revenues are large enough to cover all fixed and variable expenses, and the business has the potential to generate sustainable profits.

breakeven unit volume The number of units sold that corresponds to the number of units that must be sold to reach the breakeven point. Also called *breakeven volume* and *breakeven point volume.*

C

cash basis accounting A method of accounting that records when cash comes in from customer payments and when cash goes out to pay bills; revenues and expenses do not get captured on the Net Income Statement until a cash transaction is made.

Cash Flow Statement The financial document that measures the flow of cash in and out of your business; the Ending Cash for one month becomes the Beginning Cash for the following month.

Cash In The line on your Cash Flow Statement that captures all the cash coming into the business. Also called *Cash Received*.

Cash Out The line on your Cash Flow Statement that captures all the cash going out of the business to pay expenses. Also called *Cash Expenses*.

Collateral An asset that is pledged against a loan; it can be liquidated if the business defaults on the loan.

Cost of Goods Sold (COGS) A direct variable cost made up of the expenses associated with manufacturing, purchasing, or delivering a product or a service; it includes your direct materials and direct labor costs. See also *unit cost*.

credit lines payable Typically, revolving lines of credit that can be used in part or in full; as the money gets paid back, the credit line opens up again.

credit sales Sales transactions where the client receives the good or service and is extended payment terms to pay the bill with cash or a cash equivalent at some point in the future.

current assets Cash (in a bank account, money market account, or CD), accounts receivable (money owed the business), and inventory that can be converted into cash within 12 months.

current liabilities Obligations on the part of the business that need to be paid within 12 months; includes accounts payable, notes payable, and credit lines payable.

current ratio A measure of short-term liquidity that will tell you if there's enough accessible cash in the business to pay short-term obligations:

Current Ratio =
Total Current Assets ÷ Total Current Liabilities

D

Depreciation A portion of the total expense of an asset that is deducted each year over the useful life of the asset until the total original cost is accounted for.

E

earnings before taxes (EBT) Earnings from operations *before* federal, state, and local taxes are paid.

Ending Cash The amount of cash in a business's account at the end of the month, after payments received have been added and expenses paid have been deducted from Beginning Cash; one month's Ending Cash becomes the following month's Beginning Cash.

equity investment Capital that a business owner has put into the business at start-up, and sometimes later as well; it appears on the Balance Sheet, under owner's equity.

F

financial dashboard The three gauges you need to understand to manage a business—your Net Income Statement, your Cash Flow Statement, and your Balance Sheet; they provide critical information about how much profit the business is generating, how much cash you have in the bank to run the business, and the overall health of the business at a particular point in time.

fixed assets Assets that can take longer than 12 months to convert into cash, such as buildings, land, equipment, computers, and furniture.

fixed expenses Expenses that do not change with fluctuations in sales volume, such as rent and insurance.

forecasted demand The amount of a product or service that you predict customers are going to buy.

G

going concern A well-run, self-sustaining business that isn't under threat of bankruptcy; it has predictable revenue streams, reasonable expenses, and adequate cash levels to pay its bills now and in the foreseeable future.

good will An asset that occasionally appears on the Balance Sheet, reflecting with the monetary value of a brand name.

gross An adjective used in accounting—gross margin, gross profits, gross receipts, gross revenues—to mean *before* expenses or discounts are deducted.

gross margin The gross profit available to pay all your operating expenses; it is calculated by deducting COGS from net revenues.

gross margin percentage A formula that shows what percentage of every net revenue dollar is gross margin—that is, profit before expenses.

Gross Margin Percentage =
Gross Margin ÷ Net Revenue × 100

I

Income Statement See *Net Income Statement.*

interest expense The amount of interest paid on a short-term debt, such as a loan or a credit line.

inventory Product manufactured or purchased but not yet sold; its value as an asset is assessed as the amount it took to manufacture or purchase it.

investor's draw See *owner's draw.*

L

liabilities What the business owes, that is, obligations it needs to pay either now or in the future.

M

mortgage A long-term liability that is typically paid back, with interest, over several decades.

N

net An adjective used in accounting—net revenues, net expenses, net income—to mean *after* certain expenses have been accounted for.

net income The amount of money the business has retained after all expenses (COGS and other variable and fixed expenses) and taxes have been paid. Also called *net profit* and *bottom line.*

Net Income Statement The financial statement that reveals whether a business is generating a profit, breaking even, or showing a loss. Also called *Income Statement, Profit and Loss Statement,* and *P&L.*

net margin Net revenue minus both direct variable expenses (COGS) and indirect variable expenses (operating costs) *per unit.*

net margin ratio The relationship between your net revenue and your net income; it expresses the relationship between the top line and the bottom line on your Net Income Statement.

$$\text{Net Margin Percentage} =$$
$$\text{Net Income} \div \text{Net Revenue} \times 100$$

net revenue The value of what you've sold for that month, less any discounts you may have offered customers. Also called *net revenues.*

net 30 days A statement of terms of payment meaning payment is due within 30 days after the order is placed.

net worth See *owner's equity.*

notes payable Short-term obligations to investors, suppliers, or the bank; the proceeds from the note are typically used to cover cash crunches or to build inventory and must be paid within 12 months.

O

overdraft protection A credit line on a checking account that must be satisfied every month; it's a liability or an obligation of the business until it has been paid.

owner's draw Money that owners of businesses structured as sole proprietors and partnerships can legally pay themselves apart from salary; it's considered income and the recipient must pay income taxes on it. Also called *investor's draw*.

owner's equity The monetary value of a business; it is the difference between what your business owns and what it owes. Also called *net worth* and *shareholder equity*.

P

payables See *accounts payable*.

Profit and Loss Statement (P&L) See *Net Income Statement*.

Q

quick ratio An estimate of the short-term liquidity of a business; it's a conservative variation on the current ratio that removes the value of inventory from current assets.

$$\text{Quick Ratio} =$$
$$(\text{Cash} + \text{Accounts Receivable}) \div \text{Total Current Liabilities}$$

R

real demand The amount of a product or service that customers actually buy.

receivables See *accounts receivable*.

retained earnings The total of all the net income that has been generated by the business since its inception minus any dividends or owner's or investor's draw that have been paid out since inception.

S

salaries payable Money that has been earned by the employees but not paid yet by the business.

shareholder's equity See *net worth*.

sunk cost An expense that has yielded no benefit and can never be recovered.

T

terms of payment The date full payment is due and under what conditions a discount may be taken.

U

unit cost The direct cost of materials and labor required to create a saleable product whether that product has been sold or not. See also *cost of goods sold*.

V

variable expenses Expenses that vary based on sales volume, such as sales commissions, marketing expenses, and the like.

W

working capital Current assets minus current liabilities.

INDEX

ABOUT THE AUTHOR

Dawn Fotopulos is on a mission to prevent small business bankruptcies. A business management expert with a 20-year track record of turning around failing businesses, she has taught thousands of small business owners how to thrive in any economy through her classes, workshops, and award-winning blog, www.bestsmallbiz help.com.

Dawn is currently Associate Professor of Business at The King's College in New York City. She has been a visiting professor at New York University's Stern School of Business and Columbia Business School. She is also a Kauffman Fast Trac certified facilitator, a speaker for the National Association for Women Business Owners, Savor the Success, In Good Company, and a veteran panel moderator for the *New York Times*/AMEX Small Business Summit conferences. In addition, she is a CEO leader for The Job Creators Alliance started by Bernie Marcus, former CEO of Home Depot, to promote small business formation and profitability.

Dawn has published more than 500 articles and numerous white papers on the Cox Small Business Network, Forbes Small

Business Exchange, and Fran Tarkenton's Small Biz Club.com, as well as appearing as a guest expert on MSNBC's "Your Business" and Mitch Schlimer's "Let's Talk Business" radio show.

She holds a Bachelor of Science degree from Cornell University, and an MBA in Management with distinction from New York University's Stern School. She has held senior positions at Citicorp and Grant Street Partners, LLC, a real estate development company, and is the President of DF Consulting, Inc., a small business consultancy.

Dawn lives in New York City and can be reached at dfotopulos@ gmail.com.

BEST-SELLERS FROM AMACOM

People Styles at Work...and Beyond
ISBN: 9780814413425 (print)   9780814413432 (ebook)

At work, and in other spheres of life, how well you relate with others affects your ability to get things done. What you may not realize is that all people exhibit one of several different behavioral "styles," which determine how they think, make decisions, communicate, manage time and stress, and deal with conflict. By understanding which "people style" you're dealing with, you can establish rapport with someone more easily, become more persuasive, and avoid miscommunication and the possibility of rubbing someone the wrong way.

Success Under Stress
ISBN: 9780814432129 (print)   9780814432136 (ebook)

From overflowing priority lists to power-hungry colleagues to nagging parental guilt, stress is the defining characteristic of most of our lives. Real help is here—an all-encompassing, stress-busting tool kit that goes far beyond breathing exercises and visualization techniques. Such one-size-fits-all methods are no match for the stressors we experience daily in our overcomplicated lives.

Just Listen: Discover the Secret to Getting Through to Absolutely Anyone

ISBN: 9780814414033 (print)   ISBN: 9780814414040 (ebook)

Barricades between people become barriers to success, progress, and happiness; so getting through is not just a fine art, but a crucial skill. *Just Listen* gives you the techniques and confidence to approach the unreachable people in your life, and turn frustrating situations into productive outcomes and rewarding relationships